| WHAT KIND OF READER ARE YOU? | Do you find yourself reading only one word at a time? Do you frequently have to go back over a passage to get its meaning? |

Do your lips move when you read "silently"? *OR* do you "sound" each word in your mind? Does it take you more than a minute to read a page of an average novel?

No matter what your present difficulties are, this book can help you. Through a series of short, easy-to-take tests, *Faster Reading Self-Taught* will show you *exactly* what is wrong with your reading. Then—once you become aware of your weaknesses—a simple five-step plan will help you eliminate them.

Four books by Harry Shefter—on spelling, usage, writing, and this one on reading—were selected as the best of their kind by an educator writing in the *English Journal,* official publication of the National Council of Teachers of English.

Books by Harry Shefter

Faster Reading Self-Taught
Shortcuts of Effective English
Six Minutes a Day to Perfect Spelling

Published by POCKET BOOKS

Most Pocket Books are available at special quantity discounts for bulk purchases for sales promotions, premiums or fund raising. Special books or book excerpts can also be created to fit specific needs.

For details write the office of the Vice President of Special Markets, Pocket Books, 1230 Avenue of the Americas, New York, New York 10020.

Faster Reading
Self-Taught

Harry Shefter

PUBLISHED BY POCKET BOOKS NEW YORK

Another *Original* publication of POCKET BOOKS

POCKET BOOKS, a division of Simon & Schuster, Inc.
1230 Avenue of the Americas, New York, N.Y. 10020

ISBN: 0-671-50276-X

First Pocket Books printing of this revised edition February, 1981

10 9 8 7 6 5 4 3

POCKET and colophon are registered trademarks
of Simon & Schuster, Inc.

Printed in the U.S.A.

Acknowledgments

For permission to reprint material controlled by them, the author thanks the following authors, publishers, and agents:

Robert Bird for "How to Write Successful Ads." Reprinted by permission of the author.

Chicago Daily News for "But Can You Stay in Love?" by Sydney J. Harris.

The Continental Magazine for an excerpt from "The Super Salmon Fishing of Iceland," by Nils Anderson, copyright, Ford Motor Company.

Edwards & Deutsch for "Academy Awards"; "Jai Alai . . ."; "The King's Hunter"; "120—And Like It!" by Jack Mabley; "Slow, Slow—Quick, Quick," by George Duke; and "Spills Thrills!" from *Rocket Circle*.

Esquire, Inc. for "The Anatomy of a Sneeze," by Madelyn Wood, reprinted from *Coronet*, and "The Incredible Crab," by Reed Millard, reprinted from *Coronet*, copyright, by Esquire, Inc.

The Florida Times-Union for "Peck of Trouble Looms in Abandoning Bushel," an editorial.

Guide Publications, Inc., Plymouth, Massachusetts, for "Clever Young Man from Old Chatham," "Fables and Foibles," and "Kids, Goats, and Bees" from *Cape Cod Guide*.

The Mutual Benefit Life Insurance Co. for "Causes and Curses of Snowblindness," "Crank Her Up Again," "Down Your Alley," "For a Polite Dog," "Got a Match?" "Misguided Missiles," "Sea Farmers," "The Story of 30,000,000 Christmas Trees," and "To Shave or Not to Shave" from *Good Property*.

The New York Times for "Topics of the Times," by Lewis Nichols.

NRTA Journal for excerpts from "Why Is Leap Year?" by Raymond Schuessler.

Playbill, Inc. for "Traveling with a Camera," by John Ryan. Reprinted by permission of the author and *Playbill* Magazine.

Howard N. Seltzer for "The Letter." Reprinted by permission of the author.

Stephen M. Seltzer for "Death." Reprinted by permission of the author.

Franklin Watts, Inc. and *Pocket Books, Inc.* for the excerpt from *The Science Book of Wonder Drugs,* by Donald G. Cooley. Copyright, by Franklin Watts, Inc.

Table of Contents

CHAPTER 1

Speed Reading—Fact or Fiction?

Yes, you *can* teach yourself to read faster than you have been reading—and with better understanding! But how much faster? Are we talking about many thousands of words-per-minute, as advertised by certain commercial "reading institutes" or reported by some university research groups? Before answering the questions, let's analyze a few of the amazing claims:

- One course boasted that its graduates average 5,000 *wpm* (words-per-minute), many reach 10,000 *wpm,* and a 20-year-old university student mastered the "incredible pace of 40,000 *wpm* with increased comprehension."

- A southern college reported an experiment with the top 25 boys and 45 girls (ages 8-13 and grades 4-9) in several elementary schools. The students spent one hour a day in class learning rapid reading techniques and one hour a day at home practicing. At the beginning, the average rate was 254 *wpm.* After five weeks, the rate had climbed to 13,244 *wpm,* with 86% comprehension! One student attained a rate of 87,840 *wpm,* 90% comprehension.

- Another program announced that it had taught a five-year-old girl to read 6,000 *wpm;* a junior high school girl, 50,000 *wpm;* and an eleven-year-old boy, 123,000 *wpm!*

Have the numbers made your head spin? Do the claims seem rather wild? Here is a sampling of what some highly respected authorities think of the extraordinary rates supposedly achieved by students of speed reading courses:

- A researcher took alternate lines from two magazines, combined them into sheer nonsense paragraphs on a single page, and invited "speed readers" to test their rates. To make sure they understood the contents, all reread the passage twice. Despite the triple reading, they claimed average rates of 1700 *wpm.* But, reported the researcher, after they were told how the contents of the page had been scrambled, "I heard no more from these men about how fast they could read."

- Various researchers have given *new materials* to graduates of speed reading courses. None have been able to match the advertised wpm rates when tested for comprehension as well as speed.

- Actual photographs have been taken of eye movements during reading. On the basis of these studies, some experts have concluded that it is impossible to read more than 800-900 *wpm* with thorough understanding, if the material is unfamiliar and somewhat more complicated than light fiction.

- In all fairness, it should be noted that several authorities have said that it is possible to read thousands of wpm. The eyes and mind, however, must be trained to handle a page of print in much the way they operate when watching a motion picture. Each page then becomes similar to a single frame of a motion picture and is absorbed as a symbol of meaning rather than a collection of words. More will be said about this technique when *subvocalization* is discussed.

Now, to get a little order out of the confusion of claims and counterclaims, we will examine some facts. In this book, a page that has solid text—no diagrams, charts, or pictures—contains about 350 words. To read 1,000 *wpm,* you would have to cover three pages in one minute; for 5,000 *wpm,* 15 pages; for 10,000 *wpm,* 30 pages; and for 123,000 *wpm* (as was claimed for that eleven-year-old boy), more than 350 pages in one minute!

Let's try an experiment so that you can evaluate one aspect of speed reading first hand. Place a watch with a second hand on a table before you. *When you are told to do so,* grasp the upper right hand corner of the first page of this book and wait until the second hand of your watch has reached the number 12. At this point, you will start turning the pages as fast as you can. *You will just turn the pages; you will make no effort to read!* You must turn each page separately. If you grab several pages at once, you will have to separate them individually. You will turn pages for 60 seconds; then stop. Are you ready? *Begin turning pages!*

How many pages were you able to turn in one minute —40, 50, 60? Most people can manage 50-60 pages in the time allowed. All right, we will look at a few more facts.

Each page has two sides. If you turned 50 pages, you actually covered 100 pages of print. At 350 words per page, you turned pages at the rate of 35,000 *wpm.* Remember: you were just turning pages. You were not reading.

Our experiment has proved at least one thing to you. For most people, it is physically impossible to turn pages fast enough—*even without reading*—to cover 50,000, or 60,000, or 100,000 *wpm*. Obviously, some of the claims cited earlier are clearly preposterous. Surely, if so-called rapid readers had been asked to turn the pages *and read with even a minimum of sense,* the rate would have been sharply reduced. If one were to spend one second per page reading easy material, at most the rate would be 21,000 *wpm*.

How many people can absorb the contents of a page in one second well enough to answer questions on main ideas and details? At five seconds per page—still an unbelievable speed—the rate would drop to about 4,000 *wpm*. Doubtless, a few persons who have unique quickness of eye and mind, perhaps five in a million, can read thousands of words per minute if they have been trained or have trained themselves in the techniques of superrapid reading. It is said that Thomas Babington Macaulay, the nineteenth-century essayist, had a photographic mind, could glance at a page and exercise almost total recall. The late President Kennedy is supposed to have read fiction, newspapers, and routine reports at the rate of 2,000 *wpm*.

If few people can develop spectacular reading rates and there is disagreement among authorities about speed reading, you may wonder whether increasing your reading rate is a good idea after all. On one point, all the experts agree. Faster reading—within limits—not only saves time but unquestionably improves your understanding of what you read.

How much faster, then, should you try to train yourself to read? Unless you discover, as you learn the program and practice faithfully, that you are one of those rare persons who can absorb the contents of a page in a few seconds, you would be wise to set your sights at realistic levels. Simply put, if you can eventually read at 500 *wpm* comfortably when the material warrants it, you will be doing better than 99% of the population.

The last statement brings up another question. Why didn't I refer to "average rate" in defining your objective?

CHAPTER II

More About Reading Rate

Considering the variety of your reading activities it can be said quite emphatically that *there is no such thing as an average rate*. No single reading speed can possibly suit all your needs. Too many factors influence your reading performance at any given moment to permit you to proceed at a uniform rate at all times.

Type of Material

Nowadays many items can be bought in knockdown kits. It might take you several hours to read, understand, and follow the instructions on the "how to assemble" page that ordinarily comes with a do-it-yourself project. If you have ever tried to put together a model airplane or car, a playground swing or garden cart, a piece of furniture or children's toy, you will readily agree that your reading rate at the time might have been reduced to 5 or 10 *wpm*. In fact, sometimes if you tried to go much faster, you botched the job!

Moreover, when you tackled a new subject in school, like advanced math or a science or automobile mechanics, you found the textbook heavy going at first. You took your time doing your assignments—and rightly so—to make sure you understood. On the other hand, you were able to do the required reading in other subjects like English or social studies infinitely faster. Obviously, the type of material you are reading can and should determine your reading rate.

Familiarity with Contents

A skilled mechanic can whip through a section of a service manual in seconds. A political science professor can race through the chapters of a new book on government, as can an experienced surgeon through a medical journal. A fiction editor may need only an hour or so to reach a preliminary decision on a 400-page novel by an aspiring young writer. Those of us who know little about auto engines, politics, anatomy, or literary criticism cannot do as well with the same material as is handled so easily by a specialist in the field.

The amount of prior knowledge you bring to the type of material you are reading—its general subject matter as well as its particular vocabulary—can act as a stimulus to or a brake on your reading speed. It is reasonable to assume that at least some of the reported readers of thousands of words-per-minute were tested on pre-read or extremely familiar materials.

Motivation or Mood

In Chapter IX, you will find a detailed discussion of the tendency of most of us to function below our full potential. It is more than likely, therefore, that you already have the latent ability to read much faster than you normally do. What you need most of all is the inner drive, the persistent desire to improve your reading rate. The fact that you have decided to work with this book is a good indication that you want to become a better reader. If you need proof that you can, you will find it in the very next chapter. By completing a simple exercise, you will note how an increased reading rate, at least temporarily, can be achieved in less than five minutes!

There are times, however, when your attitude or your reaction to personal problems can create barriers to progress. How often have you found yourself staring at the same page for long minutes, struggling over material you *have* to read for some reason even though you are not in the mood for sitting in a chair with a book in your hands? Clearly, your emotional approach to reading can have a strong influence on rate.

Purpose

Suppose someone hands a book to you and tells you it has several torrid love scenes in it. Even if you are not especially interested in reading the book, you may, like many of us, want to satisfy your curiosity about the racy passages. You begin to flip pages rapidly until a significant word or phrase catches your eyes. Then you slow down! If you have ever gone through this kind of search, you may not have realized it at the time, but you were, in a sense, reading at an enormously swift pace until you reached the section of interest. In such an instance, your *purpose* in reading determined your rate.

Similarly, when you look for a name in a phone book, your eyes travel down the page, not really being conscious of all the names. When you get close to the proper alphabetical sequence, again you slow down to pinpoint your target. We will discuss such reading activities at greater length in the chapter on *skimming*.

In contrast, if you were a proofreader for a publisher, you would painstakingly focus on every word to check spelling and grammatical constructions. Your *purpose* here would slow you to a crawl. In general, then, reading for locating a particular piece of writing calls for one speed, reading for pure enjoyment calls for another, and reading for study, evaluation, or gathering complex information, still another.

Additional factors that can influence reading rate need be mentioned only briefly:

- the size of type on a printed page
- the amount of light available
- the presence of distractions
- poor eyesight, either ignored or undetected
- even the angle at which you hold the reading matter

Your first step toward improvement, therefore, is the simple recognition of the need for *flexibility* in your reading habits. Any talk of an average rate must be limited to material that is fairly familiar to you or suitable for recreational reading—for example, articles in a news digest magazine based on the daily papers you have been reading all week; fiction, biography, general magazine articles; or anything else that will not require overly careful attention. It is for such materials that you should try to develop a steady rate of about 500 *wpm,* the equivalent of roughly 100 pages an hour of a book this size. You should learn to read much faster, certainly, in subject areas where you are a specialist, in the search for a specific part of a whole selection, or in skimming for detailed information.

Finally, you should be satisfied to *read at slow rates any time you want to or need to*—depending on your purpose or the nature of the material. If you happen to enjoy a fiction writer's style and wish to savor his language dexterity, there is no reason to feel guilty about moving along at a leisurely pace. You may even be moved to reread certain passages. No one stands behind you with a whip in hand!

The key word, to repeat, is *flexibility*—slow when desirable or necessary, faster when enjoyment or casual information is the aim, and fastest when purpose and material make it possible.

As one authority put it:

> The reader who reads well adapts his reading to whatever he is reading. This is the mark of a skilled reader. . . . He instinctively puts himself in the attitude-set of the author and reads slowly or rapidly, emotes or catalogs, according to the material he is reading. . . . Varying reading attack to suit the material is the name of the game.

At this point, the next question arises. If you are to learn to read certain materials faster than you are now reading them—*faster than what?* That's what we will find out by asking you, in the next chapter, to test yourself. We will discover not only your current reading rate but also possible causes for any problems you may have. In our tests, we will use only excerpts that are suited to the kind of reading you do most of the time. References to words-per-minute will relate to the speed good readers can use when the material suggests a rate that is neither very fast nor quite slow. Incidentally, in one of the tests you will discover that, simply by an act of willpower, you will be able to increase your reading speed in less than five minutes!

CHAPTER III

Test Yourself!

The object of this self-analysis is to reveal your current strengths and weaknesses in reading. Make no special effort to do well unless the instructions request that you do so. The idea is to perform as naturally as you can so that you can get a true picture of your abilities.

You will need a pad of paper, some pencils, and a watch with a sweep second hand, or, preferably, a stopwatch. Select a place where you can work undisturbed, seat yourself comfortably before a table, and make certain you have adequate light.

TEST I

As you read this paragraph, please do exactly as I say. Place your fingers lightly on your lips. Now, continue to read. Are your lips moving? Concentrate your attention on your tongue. Is it absolutely at rest, or is it attempting to help form letters of words you are supposed to be reading silently? Now place your thumb and forefinger on your Adam's apple. Do you feel any vibration? Are you unconsciously sounding some words?

The next part of this test in rather difficult. You will have to try to continue reading and at the same time

11

analyze what your mind is doing. Ready? As you read this sentence, determine whether your mind is *repeating to itself one word at a time*. That is, are you actually reading aloud in your mind, even though not a sound is coming out of your mouth?

If you answered *Yes* to any of the questions, you are in the habit of placing mechanical or mental obstacles along your path of reading, setting up *roadblocks* that interfere with your potential ability to read faster.

TEST II

Before you take this test, it is important that you understand the instructions clearly. Holding your head absolutely still, look first to the left and then to the right. Only your eyes should have moved, not your head. Now keep your eyes fixed and move your head up and down. The purpose here is to remind you that your head and your eyes can move independently of each other.

In reading the selection that follows, you are to keep your eyes motionless (but don't strain) and allow only your head to travel down the page. You must try to read the entire group of words on each line in one glance! Do not let your eyes jump from left to right, from one word to another. If you concentrate and exert your will power, you should be able to read the selection as you have been directed.

> Once a man believes
> that he has
> achieved perfection,
> once he loses
> the motivation to do better,
> he may as well
> stop living.

He has nothing more
to contribute.
This constant urge
to do better,
to accomplish more,
is the priceless asset
of the truly
self-motivated person.
It is one of the things
that make him
colorful, dramatic,
a profitable user of time.

Were you able to control your eye movements? If you were, you have an ability that is the most important factor in any effort to increase your reading speed. If you found it impossible to prevent your eyes from hopping from one word to the next, you will need extensive drill in the material presented later, designed to eliminate word-by-word reading.

TEST III

You will recall that I said it would be possible for you to improve your reading speed to some extent in less than five minutes. This third test, therefore, has a twofold purpose. It will enable you to determine your current rate and will demonstrate that you can read faster than you generally do without any more instruction than the suggestion that you *try* to do so.

Here is an article selected from a magazine. You will read it in two parts. In the first half which follows, read as you normally would, but time yourself as you do. Count the actual number of minutes and seconds it takes you to complete reading the paragraphs.

Remember, read this part of the article at your normal reading speed. As soon as you're ready to time yourself you may start.

The Anatomy of a Sneeze

BY MADELYN WOOD

When a 13-year-old Virginia girl started sneezing, her parents thought it was merely a cold. But when the sneezes continued for hours, they called in a doctor. Nearly two months later the girl was still sneezing, thousands of times a day, and her case had attracted world-wide attention.

Hundreds of suggestions, ranging from "put a clothespin on her nose" to "have her stand on her head," poured in. But nothing did any good. Finally, she was taken to Johns Hopkins Hospital where Dr. Leo Kanner, one of the world's top authorities on sneezing, solved the baffling problem with miraculous speed.

He used neither drugs nor surgery for, curiously enough, the clue for the treatment was found in an ancient superstition about the amazing bodily reaction we call the sneeze. It was all in her mind, he said, a view which Aristotle, some 3,000 years earlier, would have agreed with heartily.

Dr. Kanner simply gave a modern psychiatric interpretation to the ancient belief that an excessive amount of sneezing was an indication that the spirit was troubled; and he proceeded to treat the girl accordingly.

"Less than two days in a hospital room, a plan for better scholastic and vocational adjustment, and reassurance about her unwarranted fear of tuberculosis quickly changed her from a sneezer to an ex-sneezer," he reported.

Sneezing has always been a subject of wonder, awe and puzzlement. Dr. Kanner has collected literally thousands of superstitions concerning it. The most universal one is the custom of invoking the blessing of the Deity when a person sneezes—a practice Dr. Kanner traces back to the ancient belief that a sneeze was an indication the sneezer was possessed of an evil spirit. Strangely, people the world over still continue the custom with the traditional, "God bless you," or its equivalent.

When physiologists look at the sneeze, they see a remarkable mechanism which, without any conscious help from you, takes on a job that has to be done. When you need to sneeze you sneeze, this being nature's ingenious way of expelling an irritating object from the nose. The object may be a speck of dust, a dash of pollen or a growth of microbes in the nose which nature is striving to remove from the nasal membranes.

A study of the process reveals that the irritation sets up a series of reactions with incredible swiftness. At the instant of irritation, the tongue moves against the soft palate and the air pressure, built up, unable to escape through the mouth, blasts its way out through the nose. A sneeze is thus quite literally an explosion of air.

(450 words—app.)

Jot down immediately the total time it took you to read this portion of the selection.

Now check your time with the data presented in the chart below. First, locate the time it took you in the first two columns at the left; then read the number in the column to the right and you will have the words-per-minute score:

WORDS-PER-MINUTE CHART

Minutes	Seconds	Wds/Min	Minutes	Seconds	Wds/Min
1	0	450	1	50	245
1	5	415	1	55	235
1	10	385	2	0	225
1	15	360	2	5	215
1	20	335	2	10	205
1	25	315	2	15	200
1	30	300	2	25	185
1	35	285	2	35	175
1	40	270	2	45	165
1	45	255	2	55	155

(Approximate)

If you finished the passage in less than 1 minute, you are reading at a rate that is far above the average and you have little to worry about. However, if it took you more than 3 minutes, you are reading exceedingly slowly—at less than half the average rate for this kind of material. You will have a lot of work to do to increase your speed.

Now, in the second half of the article I should like you to do the following as you read:

Decide, now, that you are going to read as fast as you can *even if you miss a word or two here or there!*

Try not to look at each word separately, but keep your eyes running rapidly across each line, scooping up the words in bunches.

Push yourself. Remember, you are racing against the second hand on your watch. Of course, don't go so fast that you fail to understand what you are reading.

Get your watch set! GO!

The MIT sneeze detectives found that the violent explosiveness of a sneeze can project up to 4,600 particles into the air at "muzzle velocities" of 152 feet a second. Some particles were expelled at even greater speeds—perhaps as high as 300 feet a second. The velocity is often sufficient to hurl heavier particles a distance of 12 feet.

The moisture sheath around an expelled particle evaporates, leaving a tiny nucleus which remains floating in the air. English researchers have found as many as 4,000 such particles floating there half an hour after the occurrence of the sneeze which precipitated them.

These particles are not simply harmless drops of water or inert matter. Investigators found that out by setting up, opposite a sneezer, a vertical plate coated with a culture medium favorable to the development of bacteria. By a count of bacteria growing on the plate, a single droplet has been found to create 19,000 colonies of bacteria. Thus a single sneeze can distribute more than 85,000,000 bacteria. No wonder medicine is convinced that the sneeze plays a major role in the spread of disease.

Historically, it is known that the excessive amount of sneezing involved in the influenza epidemic of 1918 helped make it the horror that it was. The Great Plague of the Middle Ages, which wiped out whole populations overnight, was helped in its spread the same way. Bubonic-plague-infected fleas, carried by rats, bit people whose lungs became infected with the pneumonic form of the disease. Then these people sneezed, spreading the plague with shocking swiftness.

Medical men say there should be a change in the way we cover a sneeze. Put your hand over your mouth, for instance, and what happens? Some of the particles, as shown by the high-speed photographs, shoot out beyond the hand, or are deflected upward to be left floating in the air. A handkerchief or tissue works far more effectively, if you have time to get one out and in place before you sneeze.

But, with or without handkerchief, the advice of an official publication of the AMA is: "When you feel a sneeze coming on, turn your head and sneeze downwards." Some authorities contend that, if we bent not only the head but the whole body in a deep bow, much of the harm done by sneezes could be avoided.

The explanation is revealed by those tell-tale photographs. The particles expelled by the sneeze are hurled toward the floor, to which they adhere, and never get a chance to become airborne and thus inhaled by others.

Sneezing in this scientific way may not provide a cure, but it could be an important weapon in medicine's battle against the common cold.

(470 words—app.)

Now jot down immediately the total time it took you to read this part of the selection.

Before going any further, let's make sure you understood what you read, even though you tried to go faster than you generally do. From the following statements, select the one in each group that you think accurately reflects an idea mentioned in the selection:

1. ___ a. Sneezing cannot spread disease.
   ___ b. Sneezing can spread disease rapidly.
   ___ c. There is no evidence that sneezing can or cannot spread disease.

2. ___ a. Particles lose their effect in less than a minute.

___ b. Particles remain in the air as long as a half hour after they have been expelled.

___ c. Particles quickly travel upward and out of reach of other people in the area of the sneeze.

3. A single sneeze can distribute as many bacteria as:

___ a. 4,600

___ b. 19,000

___ c. 85,000,000

4. ___ a. No matter how you sneeze, the effects are the same.

___ b. The best way to sneeze is to hold your hand over your mouth.

___ c. The least danger occurs when you sneeze with a deep bow, head down.

ANSWERS: 1. b, 2. b, 3. c, 4. c.

Check your time and speed in the chart below.

WORDS-PER-MINUTE CHART					
Minutes	Seconds	Wds/Min	Minutes	Seconds	Wds/Min
1	0	470	1	50	255
1	5	435	1	55	245
1	10	400	2	0	235
1	15	375	2	5	225
1	20	350	2	10	215
1	25	330	2	15	210
1	30	315	2	25	195
1	35	300	2	35	180
1	40	285	2	50	165
1	45	270	3	0	155
(Approximate)					

Now let's take stock. The second selection is about 20 words longer than the first, but you probably read it as much as 25 per cent faster because of your strong effort to do so. And if you got the answers right, you also proved to yourself that you lost very little in comprehension. Let me point out that the questions are not easy ones but represent what you would normally be expected to derive from the contents of the article.

If you were unable to read the second selection faster than the first, there is no need for discouragement. Work hard on Chapters V, VI, and IX. Then come back to this test. You will probably read both parts with greater speed than you did before.

TEST IV

The short paragraphs below are provided to help you test your ability to separate main ideas from details. To the right of each paragraph are questions. In each set, the first question is based on the main idea and the others on details.

Read each paragraph carefully *once!* Then, of the five choices offered, check the number of the answer that best completes the statement at the beginning of the question. Note that 2 points are assigned to "main idea" and 1 point to "detail" answers. The total is 10 for the three paragraphs.

a. Propaganda is the most terrible weapon so far developed. It is worse than poison gas. If the wind is in the right direction, gas may kill a few and injure others; but the possibilities of manipulating the public mind by withholding or discoloring

The title below that best expresses the ideas of this paragraph is
1. Propaganda or poison gas
2. The threat of propaganda
3. Control of facts

the facts are appalling. One is so helpless in the face of it. No one can think intelligently without knowing the facts; and if the facts are controlled by interested men, the very idea of democracy is destroyed and becomes a farce.

4. How to detect propaganda
5. Propaganda in a democracy .... ( )

Manipulating the public mind by controlling the facts is a denial of
1. interest
2. intelligence
3. democracy
4. directions
5. help .... ( )

b. Though the pain from a scorpion's sting is intense and may endure for several hours, there is little danger of serious and lasting injury. The scorpion is a sinister-looking creature, with an armored, segmented body supported by eight legs. It possesses numerous eyes, yet for all practical purposes it is devoid of vision, with only monstrous, fingerlike pincers to guide it. These pincers are powerful weapons with which the scorpion seizes and crushes its prey. The jointed tail, with its poison needle point, can be wielded with deadly accuracy if the pincers are not effective. Sinister as is the scorpion in the insect world, there is no reason why it should be feared by man.

The title below that best expresses the ideas of this paragraph is
1. How the scorpion fights
2. Enemies of the scorpion
3. A forbidding ally
4. The scorpion's sting
5. Why men fear scorpions ...... ( )

The scorpion's primary threat to its prey lies in its
1. range of vision
2. speed of motion
3. armored body
4. pointed tail
5. pincers ..... ( )

Its enemies are principally insects that destroy grain fields, and in killing these pests the scorpion serves a beneficent purpose.

c. Whenever a dedicated salmon fisherman drifts into daydreams about the best setting for his sport, he is likely to conjure up visions of the kind of streams and rivers found in Iceland. His mind's eye may not see that country's wide green meadows, its long, hulking, snow-draped mountains, its glassy fjords, its people who smile as easily as they breathe, but he will imagine the water rushing over rocky falls into pools where thousands of salmon pause briefly in their late-spring and early-summer dash from the Atlantic Ocean to their upstream spawning beds. He will see himself with rod in hand floating a fly across the pool— once, twice, a few more times— feel the salmon, attack it, play the infuriated fish and eventually work it to shore. A daydream, yes, but also a fact. For sportsmen, Iceland is the greatest salmon fishing country in the world.

The title below that best expresses the ideas of this paragraph is
1. A furious fish
2. Daydreams
3. The beauty of nature
4. The best salmon fishing
5. The rivers of Iceland
...... ( )

To reach their spawning beds, salmon
1. cross the Atlantic
2. leap into pools
3. dash upstream
4. swim downstream
5. float with the tide
...... ( )

The writer's attitude toward nature seems to show
1. indifference
2. fear
3. dislike
4. forgetfulness
5. keen appreciation
...... ( )

ANSWERS: (2 points for each title, 1 for the details)
          a. 2, 3   b. 3, 5   c. 4, 3, 5

A score of 6 or below is *unsatisfactory;* 7 or 8, about *average;* 9 or 10, *superior*.

Your score should tell you how much attention you will have to pay to the exercises presented in Chapter VII. It is stating the obvious to say that the basic objective of all reading is to understand what has been written or printed. Sheer speed without comprehension is valueless!

TEST V

You can't do a satisfactory job without the proper tools. One of the most valuable tools in the job of reading is a good vocabulary. Let's see how you rate in this respect.

Below you will find a paragraph in which certain words have been omitted. Next to each blank space the definition of the missing word has been inserted in parentheses. From the list at the top of the paragraph, select the word that matches the definition and write it into the space provided. The object here is to test your vocabulary, not your powers of guessing, so select only those words that are familiar to you. There's no sense in cheating yourself.

derision	abate
elation	admonition
decorum	docile
brusque	altercations
antagonists	diminutive

An _____ (warning) to Jimmy to refrain from engaging in further _____ (fights) with the boy next door had brought little results. It is difficult to

_____ (check) the fury of young _____ (opponents), each eager to prove he is superior. A _____ (harsh) order to observe _____ (model behavior) is rarely effective with _____ (small) battlers. Accordingly, both fathers decided to use some psychology. They would greet future conflicts with _____ (scornful laughter) and praise the more _____ (gentle) of the lads. It was with _____ (great satisfaction) that the parents noted gradual progress.

ANSWERS: (in order of appearance): admonition, altercations, abate, antagonists, brusque, decorum, diminutive, derision, docile, elation.

Did the words seem too hard? Actually, they were taken from a list judged to be suitable for high school students. Similar words are used daily in newspapers, magazines, books, television programs—in every medium in which informed people write or talk. If you scored under 7, you can be sure that your limited vocabulary is a handicap to your efforts to achieve good comprehension as well as speed. The suggestions made in Chapter VIII should help you improve in this area.

Now that you have participated in the series of self-diagnostic tests, you should be able to pinpoint your particular reading weaknesses. Apart from physical or mental disability, emotional disturbance, or sight problems, we have covered the major causes of poor reading for people who have the potential to make rapid progress:

1. Certain physical obstructions, like lip movements during silent reading, can hold back speed.

2. Word-by-word reading retards rate as well as comprehension.

3. Some slow readers simply lack the drive to force themselves to develop faster rates.

4. Failure to differentiate between main ideas and minor details makes good comprehension difficult.

5. A poor vocabulary is a serious handicap in any attempt to improve reading ability.

You know which techniques you must stress in your study program and which you have fairly well in hand. You should be about ready to get to work. But one more question may be troubling you. *How long will it take you to improve?*

CHAPTER IV

How Long Will It Take?

Directors of college reading laboratories have published results indicating substantial increases in reading rate and comprehension "in a few weeks" of concentrated study. In fact, you will recall that those middle school boys and girls mentioned on the first page of this book supposedly went from 254 *wpm* to 13,244 *wpm* in five weeks! Most researchers, however, are much more modest in their claims, suggesting that definite, lasting progress can be made in eleven to fifteen weeks, with several hours each week of practice and application.

One professor came up with interesting findings. You will note that in the accompanying Graph and Table a sudden sharp dip occurs during the ninth week. Analysis revealed that the downward slide was produced because the students were anticipating a long Easter recess and had apparently lost their concentration for a while. Perhaps, too, they had grown stale and needed a break in routine. At any rate, after the class had returned to its regular sessions, the gains, as you can see, shot up dramatically. Although the total reading rate increase was 95%, the more important measure was that of *rate-comprehension.*

The "Rate of Comprehension," as indicated below, increased by almost 200%! This measure is obtained by multiplying the reading rate by the percentage of the material comprehended. For example, a person reading at 300 *wpm*, with 50% achievement on a test for comprehension, receives a *rate-comprehension* score of 150 *wpm*. This type of score has more meaning than merely *rate of reading* since it combines both speed and comprehension. It is misleading to use speed alone to reflect reading level; increase of speed without a corresponding increase in comprehension is obviously useless. Reading authorities who question the claims made by commercial reading institutes base their arguments on the *rate-comprehension* scores. As stated earlier, very few people, if any, can read at many thousands of words-per-minute without a serious loss of comprehension.

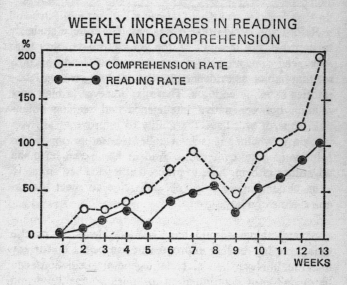

WEEKLY INCREASES IN READING RATE AND COMPREHENSION

O----O COMPREHENSION RATE
●——● READING RATE

TABLE

Weekly Increases in Reading
Rate and Comprehension

Week	Rate of Reading		Rate of Comprehension	
	WPM	% increase	WPM	% increase
1	229	0	142	0
2	234	2	181	27
3	271	18	175	23
4	283	24	184	30
5	255	11	209	47
6	287	25	239	68
7	305	33	260	83
8	336	47	225	58
9	284	24	182	28
10	342	49	251	77
11	373	63	281	98
12	409	79	293	106
13	447	95	415	192

Before you decide that it was easy for college students to improve, but it won't be for you, let me tell you this. Advanced education does not necessarily lead to good reading habits, as evidenced by the need for reading laboratories in many colleges. There is, however, a high correlation between native intelligence and reading potential. Thus, if you have the ability to improve at all, you can do it whether it is in a college classroom or in the privacy of your own room. And at home you have the advantage of being able to proceed at a pace best suited to your circumstances, with no obligation to meet the requirements of a large group.

Several things should have become clear. No precise time table for reading improvement can be set up for any individual. Nevertheless, certain general predictions can be made. Your determination to "push yourself" beyond your normal, possibly lazy, reading habits should bring the most immediate results—in a matter of several weeks at most. Your daily practice sessions, aimed at eliminating bad reading habits, should help you improve after five or six weeks.

The Graph and Table you have just examined indicate that progress does not occur at a steady pace. At one point you may make a big jump forward and at another a small one or none at all. This will be as it should be. You must not become discouraged because you are not improving as fast as you think you should. Events at home or at work may disrupt your schedule. But you cannot allow yourself to offer these interferences as reasons to give up in disgust.

You will also have your low periods, just as the students did when they were looking forward to a holiday and did not feel like working very hard. You will experience days when you can't stand another minute of drill. The sight of a printed page may turn your stomach. You may even wonder why you ever decided to improve your reading skills.

The halt in progress for brief periods can be compared to a "slump" that affects all people. The star baseball player suddenly stops hitting for a while, or the basketball player can't seem to "buy a basket" for a game or two. The writer stares at a blank page one day and cannot generate one decent word. The business executive decides he must "get away from it all" because he can't explain why he is not functioning normally. When you reach a low period, take some time off. Forget about reading rates and comprehension until you feel refreshed. Then get back to your program with renewed vigor—but get back!

Is that all there is to it? No, not really. We must be honest with each other. The daily drills will be the warmups, the practice sessions. But practice alone is not enough. You will have no measure of success in your program for reading improvement unless you apply what you have practiced to actual reading situations. You must make a deliberate effort to exercise your improving reading skills on an ever-increasing range of materials. You will have to become a *reader*—with all that is meant by the word when it is said with emphasis —a *reader* of books, newspapers, magazines. You will have to use your new skills so that they become habitual. Failure to do so will mean that you are not really serious about holding on to any improvement you may have made.

This branching out of your reading interests will, of course, take longer than the 15-minutes-a-day program outlined in Chapter X. But remember: you will not be punishing yourself by expanding the time you spend reading. You will be experiencing one of life's greatest pleasures. Soon you will be participating in the joys of reading willingly because you will be doing it well. Final success will depend on your attitude, your ability to set aside enough time to practice faithfully, and your understanding of the fact that progress will not always be smooth.

You now have some idea of how long it will take you to improve. You have also had a preview of the major causes of poor reading that can be eliminated by determined effort and sustained practice. Each of the next five chapters will focus separately on a detailed analysis of one problem area and offer specific suggestions for eliminating the undesirable reading habits associated with it. Once you know what to practice and how to go about it, you will be on your way!

THE
FIVE-STEP
PLAN

CHAPTER V

STEP ONE:

Knock Out the Roadblocks!

Handicap races are often included in outdoor field events. In one of the most popular, contestants step into large gunny sacks and hop awkwardly to the finish line. In another favorite, participants must pick up potatoes (or similar objects) in spoons and keep them balanced in the cautious dash forward. During all such events, the runners deliberately assume handicaps in the spirit of the contests.

When you read, you are not engaged in a handicap race. You want to go as fast as you can. Yet the self-tests you took may have revealed some bad habits that interfere with your reading rate, much the way sacks and potatoes can interfere with running speed. The major difference is that you have not chosen to handicap yourself voluntarily!

Many obstacles to better reading can be traced to childhood. Your earliest reading experiences were largely oral. Great stress was laid on saying words aloud, getting the feel of the sounds with your lips and tongue, and pointing to familiar objects as you identified them. This is all very good practice in the early primary grades when students are being trained to associate sounds with meaning. However, some children do not progress easily into silent reading. Whether it is caused by feelings of insecurity or just by habit, they continue to read aloud subconsciously. They follow the words with their lips, tongues, fingers, or heads because they don't trust their eyes and want to make sure they don't get lost on a page. Thus they unknowingly create obstructions to later efforts to develop satisfactory silent reading rates.

Let's explore this problem somewhat further. What your eyes see is interpreted by your mind which functions much faster than any physical activity you can perform. In reading, then, whatever you do that forces the mind to keep the same pace as a physical movement slows it up. You have seen children, learning to talk, go through a stammering stage because their minds race far ahead of the speech organs. Soon the youngsters learn that they cannot form sounds as fast as they can think them. Almost instinctively most of them adjust their speed of thought to their rate of producing understandable spoken language.

In silent reading, there is no reason to slow up your mind. Indeed, it is essential that you do not, if you want to develop speed and understanding. The less interference you give your mind as it tries to interpret what your eyes are looking at, the faster and better it operates.

We shall refer to all self-imposed obstacles to better reading as *roadblocks* to rapid and meaningful progress from one thought to the next on a page. Typical *roadblocks* will be examined in detail and suggestions will be offered for their elimination. Before we do, consider two important points:

- It is possible that your reading problems do not stem from any of the *roadblocks* we are going to discuss. Or you may discover that you have been handicapping yourself with only one or two of them. As soon as you have read the description of a particular *roadblock* and are convinced that it is not one of your bad reading habits, forget about it! In fact, skip the entire section that refers to it. You can spend your time more profitably practicing the elimination of a weakness you do possess.

- After each suggestion for improvement below, you will find sample exercises for practice. I am sure you realize that it would be impossible to include in any book all the material you will ultimately need for your full program of practice. You will have to set up additional exercises by yourself, following the style of the examples given. In most instances, this will mean that you pick random paragraphs from newspapers, magazines, or books that will provide you with the necessary drills.

A. Vocalization and Lip Reading

Description: If you are faced with these problems, you tend to make the sounds of the words in your throat during silent reading (vocalization), or you move your lips voicelessly (lip reading) as if you were reading aloud. In either case, you force your mind to absorb the material at a pace no faster than you can speak. That is not fast enough for efficient reading.

Suggestions: To make sure you know where the sounds are made in the throat, do this now. Place one finger on each side of your Adam's apple. Blow air steadily through your lips. No vibration? Right. Now hum any tune. Do you feel the buzzing effect? *That's what you want to eliminate in silent reading.* As you read the rest of this paragraph, make certain there is no vibration of any kind in your throat. If you have trouble controlling the sound, keep your fingers on your throat and blow *air* out as you read.

There are several ways of eliminating lip movements. Try these suggested procedures and select the one that suits you best.

1. Place between your lips, *not your teeth,* some object heavy enough to force you to exert pressure to hold it as you read.

2. Press your lips tightly together, and at the same time push your tongue firmly against the roof of your mouth.

3. Although I certainly don't recommend this as a permanent habit, try chewing gum with exaggerated jaw and lip movements, something like the very tough characters seen in gangster pictures.

4. Purse your lips in a whistling position and blow air out, *but make no sounds.*

Of course, you understand that you use artificial controls only as long as you think you have not yet habitually removed the roadblocks. This applies to any of the "cures" described in this chapter. In the passage below, test out each of the above recommendations, one for every two or three sentences, until you can decide on the one method you will use for later practice sessions.

For a Polite Dog

Every dog can be trained to be a well-behaved pet and an obedient one.

Your first problem is housebreaking. The owner of the famous "Lassie" accomplished it by using a large box as her home. When he couldn't watch her, he barred the exit. She soon learned if she used her living quarters improperly her keen sense of smell made the situation unpleasant. By allowing her out after every meal, her owner soon began to adjust her needs to those times. A gentle pat on the head and a tidbit told her she had done the right thing.

B. Crutches

Description: Crutches are used by people who unfortunately need extra supports. There are mental crutches, too. Suppose that as you read you are in the habit of pointing your finger at each word, or sliding a straight edge, like a ruler, from one line to the next. If so, you are using a mental crutch. You are attempting to give your mind an extra support in its efforts to concentrate. But you are also holding back your speed! To repeat, your hand cannot possibly move as fast as your mind.

Suggestion: The advice here is so simple that it may sound ridiculous to you. However, there are lots of things we do wrong only because we aren't aware that we can correct them by an obvious device. For instance, if someone told you that you make too many gestures when you talk to people, you might cure the habit very easily by putting your hands in your pockets when you speak until you have learned not to bring them forward unnecessarily. To cure finger pointing or using a ruler to guide your eyes, all you need do is hold the book, newspaper, or magazine you are reading *in both hands* until the undesirable habit is under control. Thus you fight the problem by making it impossible to arise. Before you practice, try this as a warmup. Select objects in various parts of the room. Describe their positions aloud, but remember to keep your hands at your sides.

C. Failure to Use Peripheral Vision

Description: Look directly at any object in the room you are now occupying. Let's say it is a lamp. You see the lamp, but about five or six feet to the right of it and an equal distance to the left, your eyes have also absorbed images of perhaps a chair and a picture on the wall. You definitely see all three objects even though your eyes are focused on only one of them. This ability of yours to see out of the corners of your eyes, so to speak, is what is known as *peripheral vision*. If you wanted to make a more detailed study of the chair or picture, there would be no need to move your head. By moving only your eyes, you could shift their focus to any object within the limits of their peripheral vision.

A further illustration of this point can be found in observing people at a tennis match. For those seated directly facing the center of the court, the ball passes out of peripheral vision so quickly that they must move their heads from side to side continually to watch the play. Those seated behind the players have no need to indulge in a mass exhibition of neck twisting because their eyes can take in all the action.

Similarly, a line of print very easily falls within the limits of your peripheral vision. It is true that you have to shift the focus of your eyes as they move across the line, *but you should not move your head*. Otherwise, you are setting up a roadblock as bad as finger pointing. Since your head cannot keep pace with your mind, you are decreasing your reading speed.

Suggestions: We are concerned here with the elimination of head movements as one part of training yourself to see more than one word at a time. Much more will be said about this skill in the next chapter, which concentrates on how to *read words in groups*. Therefore, do not treat the exercises below lightly. The extent to which you can learn to use peripheral vision in reading will determine the increase in speed you will eventually achieve!

Again, experiment with the techniques recommended for practice and select the one you prefer:

1. Place one finger on either side of your jaw.

    OR

2. Grab your chin as if in deep thought.

    OR

3. Place a finger on the tip of your nose.

The important thing is to check any movement of your head as you do the exercises. We will use sets of ten to illustrate how each type of exercise should be arranged. You can, and should, prepare additional sets for further practice.

WARMUP 1

Look directly at the center number on each line below, holding your head still as suggested, and try to read all three numbers as if they were a total. For example, in the first set your mind should register "one hundred thirty-nine," not "one, three, nine."

1	3	9
7	6	2
8	4	7
2	2	5
4	5	3
6	9	1
3	1	4
5	7	6
9	8	8
1	7	8

WARMUP 2

The following word groups contain phrases you have probably seen many times before. For instance, you doubtless recognize the first one, "Three Blind Mice," as the title of the well-known song, not as three isolated words. Keep your eyes focused on the center word of each phrase, identify its familiar context, move down the page, and *keep your head still*.

THREE	BLIND	MICE
THE	THREE	MUSKETEERS
HOME	SWEET	HOME
TOM	DICK	and HARRY
DOWN	THE	HATCH
FRIENDS	ROMANS	COUNTRYMEN
TICK	TACK	TOE
STAR	SPANGLED	BANNER
MISSED	THE	BOAT
SMOOTH	AS	SILK

WARMUP 3

Now read the column below, similar in line width to those found in newspapers or digest magazines. Try to "see" the whole line at once, as your eyes move down, but even if they do slide from side to side, *hold your head still!*

Everything about the porpoise could be written in superlatives. Not a fish but an air-breathing mammal, he swims incredibly fast, kills sharks, communicates with his own kind, herds fish. He has the world's best sonar equipment. One scientist believes that his brain is so similar to a human being's that he might even be taught to talk.

D. Regressions

Description: People who have this bad habit don't seem to be able to go from the end of one line to the beginning of the next without frequently going back *(regressing)* to the one just read. All of us, of course, do this sort of thing occasionally. We may want to reread a particularly good sentence or our minds are elsewhere instead of concentrating on what we are supposed to be reading. *Regressions,* however, become a serious problem when the reader finds it difficult to control them. Covering the same ground twice makes it impossible to move ahead quickly on a page.

Regressions stem, to a large extent, from lack of confidence. The reader is constantly worried that he has missed something and is, in a sense, fearful of going forward. For instance, people who are always concerned about losing things (although they rarely do!) are likely to be regressive readers. They simply must go back to check.

Suggestions: Perhaps the most important recommendation I can make here is to urge you to begin to believe in your ability to read and understand as well as most other people. Stop worrying about having missed something in a previous portion of a sentence or paragraph. Keep moving ahead steadily, regardless of any strong desire you may have to turn back, *to regress.* Added confidence will help you eliminate this tendency. Train yourself, also, as you come to the end of a line, to use your peripheral vision to sneak a look at the beginning of the next line (through the corner of your left eye).

In the following selection you will find a great mass of detail. As you read, resist the desire to go back to check each item mentioned. Get the main idea and don't feel compelled to memorize names, implements, or treatments.

Considering the implements they had, it's a wonder the ancients ever thought of shaving.

The Chimus, who came before the Incas, pulled out their stringy beards with solid gold tweezers as each new hair appeared. When they died, the tweezers were laid in the coffin.

Shavers in Africa had an even more barbarous method. Warm oil first softened the whiskers, then a "razor" in the hands of a barber literally chiseled the whiskers off.

Indians of Central and South America faced the problem in practically the same way, except they used nut shells or bamboo knives on the oil-softened beard. Other natives in Africa daubed resin on their faces, let it remain for a few minutes, then took resin, whiskers, and probably a little skin off with an oyster or clam shell.

Some hardy gentlemen of olden times removed hair from their faces by chemicals which burned rather than cut. A bone knife scraped off the residue.

Shaving came into modern use in France in the reign of Louis XIII, but it was not until the 18th century that shaving the whole beard became common.

A note for the future. As predicted by a college professor, a new bearded age has come upon us and may continue for the next decade or so.

———

If you now know that ancient shaving methods were crude and painful, you grasped the main idea of the article. You very likely can recall at least three or four of the supporting details: tweezers, chisels, oils, various shells and knives, or resin. If you had gone back in your reading several times to verify a place or implement, your understanding of the basic point would not have been increased. Admittedly, if you were studying for a test or trying to memorize a passage, you would go back over the material many times, but then you would not be using your normal reading speed anyway. You will recall that we stressed the need for flexibility in rate. Regressions should never be part of the pattern when you are reading for enjoyment and can do so with reasonable speed.

If regressions continue to trouble you, try any of the following:

1. Type several paragraphs, leaving 3 spaces between lines for the first few sentences, then 2 spaces, then 1. Subsequently, reading these paragraphs will aid you in developing a rhythmical sweep across and back from line to line.

2. Type additional paragraphs, this time with normal spacing, but use small letters for one line and all capitals for the next, alternating this way to the end of the passage. Thus you sharpen the line sequence.

3. Take a newspaper column and underline every other line before you read it. Again, you make each line stand out better and train your eyes to avoid regressions.

NOTE: An important point to remember in your efforts to control regressions is that it is not necessary to know the meaning of every word in a paragraph. Never stop in the midst of your reading to work on a word. Move right along. Usually, the context will make the meaning of strange words clear. The chapter on vocabulary will explain how to handle words you may want to learn.

E. Subvocalization

Description: It is true that most readers sound out words in their minds *(subvocalize)* to some extent. Only a few can eliminate this habit entirely, those very few whose reading rate can be measured in thousands of words-per-minute. These rare people have learned how to react to thought-impressions of entire paragraphs or pages, never concentrating on particular words or phrases. It is a skill that should be considered the ideal for most readers, one which may not be reached entirely but which represents the ultimate mastery of the reading process.

Since *subvocalization* might be termed *inner speech,* anything that resembles reading aloud holds back the mind from its full speed potential. Realistically, it is not very easy to eliminate this tendency to say words mentally as you read silently. You should understand, however, that the more you cut down on your subvocalization, the more your reading speed will increase. As you learn to focus on ever larger groups of words, rather than individual ones, the problem of subvocalization should be substantially reduced.

Suggestions: What proof is there that you can learn to read without any inner speech at all? To convince you that such reading is possible, we will experiment with a procedure used extensively in the medical profession. As you know, to build up the body's resistance, doctors sometimes give patients injections that produce mild cases of a threatening disease. We will use a somewhat similar technique. *You will be asked to subvocalize deliberately,* but in a manner that will build up your resistance to the problem in actual reading. As usual, after you have experimented with the sample selections, you will locate additional practice material in other reading sources. The basic procedure here involves a three-step process:

44

1. Keep repeating the word *NO* silently as you read the selection—*NO* for *NO SUBVOCALIZATION*.

Why do we have leap year, with its extra day? Who started it? How necessary is it? Why was the extra day jammed into February?

The reason for leap year is found in the length of a solar (tropical) year—the time it takes the earth to circle the sun—and the astronomers have worked this out as approximately 365.2422 days, or 365 days, 5 hours, 48 minutes and 46 seconds. So we have a calendar with 365 days in ordinary years, and every four years we add a leap year that picks up the extra fraction and keeps our calendar in step with the seasons. This still isn't quite exact, so we omit leap day in four centuries. The year 1600 was a leap year; the years 1700, 1800, and 1900 were not; the year 2000 will be.

You subvocalized *NO* as you read. Did you still get the point that a leap year helps to keep the calendar in step with the seasons? If you did, you have your first proof that inner speech can be eliminated.

2. Now we will try something more complicated. Surely you have memorized a short poem, "The Star-Spangled Banner," part of a speech, anything at all. As you read the next excerpt silently, *repeat in your mind any previously memorized piece!*

People have wondered why Julius Caesar inserted his quadrennial leap day in February. The explanation is simple. The Roman year in ancient times started on March 1—as indicated by the fact that we still call several months by Roman words. September means "seventh month"; October, eighth; November, ninth; and December, tenth. February was the last month of the old Roman year; the extra day was tagged onto the end of the year.

Did you get the main idea that February was chosen because it was the last month of the Roman year? NOW, A WORD OF CAUTION! Certainly your concentration suffers when you subvocalize material completely different from what you are reading. For this reason, the device we are using is definitely not recommended on a long-range basis. But you were probably amazed that, despite the interference of competing subvocalization, you were able to read reasonably well. *All we want to do here is to prove you can read without inner speech.*

During each session, after you have practiced with the first two techniques, you should immediately transfer to exercises that will train you to read with minimal subvocalization without artificial aids.

3. Cut out short, newspaper-sized columns and paste them onto 3 by 5 cards. Hold the cards exposed for a fraction of a second, just long enough for your eyes to sweep down vertically so fast that there will be very little opportunity to subvocalize. Incidentally, this technique is also useful as preparation for the work in the next chapter. The super-readers can, theoretically, absorb the meaning of the column in one glance. After you have swept down the selection, think about the main idea expressed. Then check with the original to see whether your excessive speed in reading hurt your comprehension in any way.

One of the little known facts about leap year is its connection with playing cards. Historians say that playing cards, as we know them today, are probably a direct development of small one-week Egyptian card calendars that were combined into a pack of 52, to make a complete calendar for one year. The 53rd card, now the joker, was provided to take care of the odd 365th day of the year and may have represented the 366th day of leap year.

F. Reversals

Description: Does *not* ever read *ton* to you, or does *saw* become *was* sometimes? Does what you thought was *won* turn out to be *now?* These are *reversals,* actually caused by a momentary reading from right to left, rather than the normal left to right. Such errors lead to confusion and in themselves create some of the other roadblocks we have mentioned above. It's pretty much like dropping the potato off the spoon and having to go back to pick it up again.

Reversals may be caused by brain injury or some visual defect. But if these factors are not present, the problem can be traced to a lack of familiarity *in the mind* with the structure of the word, a failure to have the "feel" of it. The design or image of the word rings the wrong bell.

Suggestion: To handle reversals, use a method that is also very effective in strengthening spelling skill. Keep a list of words that cause you trouble. From time to time spend a few minutes using the *tracing technique.*

Suppose you constantly seem to read *net* for *ten.* Write the word *ten* out on a scrap of paper. Place your *finger,* not your pen or pencil, directly on the word. Now trace the letters as you say each one aloud. Do this three times. Then turn the paper over and write the word rapidly as you pronounce your name or some other phrase. You must be able to write the word entirely automatically, without thinking about it at all. Authorities who have experimented in this field agree that if you can experience

47

the form of a word through your sense of touch you are less likely to confuse it in your mind. For a more detailed description of the tracing technique, see my book *Six Minutes a Day to Perfect Spelling,* published by Pocket Books.

So much for *roadblocks.* Fortunately, this is the area of reading disabilities where progress can be made most rapidly, with the exception of *subvocalization* as already noted. If you can substantially reduce the amount of mental speech during silent reading, good. If you don't seem to get very far at first, do the best you can and don't worry about it. Improvement will come gradually if you learn to do everything else right.

Let me caution you once more. If you are sure that some of the physical obstacles to rapid reading are not part of your problem, don't spend time on them. Concentrate on the one or two that need serious attention—and then only 2 minutes a day, according to our schedule, which will be explained in detail in Chapter X. Use any time saved in practicing other skills recommended in the program.

CHAPTER VI

STEP TWO:

Stretch Your Span!

Nobody should attempt to fix a machine unless he knows how it works. This principle can be applied to the mechanism that runs a typewriter as well as the "machine" that makes it possible for you to read. The "parts"—your eyes, mind, and emotions—are few in number, it would appear, but they function in a much more complicated manner than most people realize. For this reason, then, it is essential that you have a thorough knowledge of how your "reading machine" works before you make an effort to repair it.

How do your eyes function when you read?

The typewriter, as you know, is designed to punch out words, letter by letter. Every time you strike a key or the spacing bar, there is a stop for a fraction of a second and then the rubber-covered cylinder (the *carriage*) jumps slightly to the left. *Bear in mind that you can imprint a letter only when the carriage stops, not while it is moving!* If, for example, you were typing the following sentence, you would cause the carriage to stop and jump 34 times (27 letters, 6 spaces, 1 question mark):

Can you count the number of stops?

If you wished to increase the size of the jumps, you could set up *column stops*. These permit the carriage to slide to a given point (skipping the intervening spaces), to accept imprints, slide to the next point, and so on, as below:

| 41 | 12 | 415 |
| 36 | 28 | 218 |

Thus it is possible to create a stop for every letter, space, and punctuation mark on a line or to limit the number of stops to only a few, depending on the nature of the material being typed.

You may be somewhat surprised to learn that when you read, your eyes behave much like the carriage of a typewriter. They do not travel across a line of print in one continuous sweep, but move in the stop-and-go fashion of the machine. You can prove this immediately by getting someone to help you for a few minutes.

Ask your friend to hold a book or magazine selection about a foot in front of and above his head. Place yourself so that you can watch his eye movements. Now ask him to begin reading—but tell him to read *only the letters, one after another,* not the words. You will be observing a human "typewriter" in action. You will see the eyes leapfrog from letter to letter; they will not sweep smoothly along. You will actually be able to count the stops after a little practice.

Now ask your reader to concentrate on *words, one by one.* You will notice that the stops decrease in number and that the eyes slide a bit before they pause.

Finally, tell your friend to read as fast as he can. If he is an average reader, you will observe his eyes stop only three or four times per line. They will be operating exactly as the carriage of the typewriter does when a typist is using the column stops.

You should be convinced then that the eyes *do* stop periodically as they move across a line of print. You should also accept the fact that the more stops there are per line the slower is the rate of reading.

How does your mind function when you read?

Let us return to our typewriter comparison. We know that when a key is struck, the letter or symbol is printed on the paper at the moment contact is made with the carriage, and that each time an impression is made there is a split-second stop. Similarly, every time the eyes of a reader pause, they send an impression to the mind, which interprets it and gives it meaning. That's why, even though it sounds impossible, we say that you read while your eyes are *not moving*. Just as no letters can be typed while the carriage is in motion, so no images can be sent to the mind while the eyes are moving. You can readily understand that the more stops there are on a line, the more the total image is broken up, and consequently the more difficult it is for the mind to interpret it. Surely it is easier to study a photograph if it is presented in one piece than if it is cut up jigsaw-puzzle style.

Now, your reading mechanism has one very significant advantage over a typewriter. If you've ever watched a champion typist in action, you have seen fingers fly over the keys so rapidly that the carriage sweeps steadily to the left without any visible pauses. Even the skilled office worker, though not quite so fast, manages to operate in bursts, like bullets from a machine gun, and only three or four definite pauses are noticeable on a line. Only when you watch the "hunt and peck" artist laboriously bang out one letter at a time can you clearly see the numerous stops. The typewriter cannot be made to print whole words, however, as a printing press does. Regardless of the speed, it is impossible to strike two or more keys simultaneously without jamming the machine. Thus the speed typist creates an optical illusion by going so fast that the carriage seemingly slides along without stopping. The stops are there, whether you see them or not.

But the reader *can take in a word or more at a glance.* There is no fixed limit to the size of the image your eyes can send to your mind. Only those almost hopelessly retarded in reading stop at every letter. Even the very slow reader can manage at least a word at a time. Good readers consistently pass from one phrase to the next. A few read so fast that if you watched their eye movements you would notice hardly any pauses at all. So you can see how tremendous an advantage your reading mechanism has over the typewriter. It is the key that unlocks the secret of how to improve your reading speed.

You are not held back by the limitations of a machine. Your mind will absorb as much as you can give it within reason and within its basic ability to interpret. You are the master here. If one way to train yourself to read faster is to decrease the number of times your eyes stop on a line, it is within your powers to do so! Your problem, therefore, is not whether you *can,* but *how* to do it.

Before we tell you how, let's continue with a few more observations on how the mind operates in the process we call reading. You have learned that you read when your eyes pause and that your mind interprets what you see at that time. How much do you have to see to derive meaning? Experiments have demonstrated that only the general outlines of words and phrases are necessary for recognition. Just as you can recognize some member of your family merely by hearing his walk or seeing the back of his head, so the eyes don't need the letter-by-letter picture of a word to identify it. A glance at but one or two prominent letters may be enough. For instance, in *departmental* the *d, p, t,* and *l* may suffice to complete the signal to the mind.

In fact, it has also been clinically proved that we don't even need the whole letters to make our identification. We tend to recognize the upper parts of letters more than the lower. Take a card of some sort. Cover the lower half of the letters in a line of print. Then try reading it. Follow this by covering the upper half. You will note that you can read more easily using the first method.

If, then, the mind does not need every letter of a word to recognize it, doesn't even need the complete designs of the ones it does use, it is reasonable to conclude that there is rarely the need to look at every word to extract the meaning of a phrase. The mind can employ the pattern technique here, too. A quick glance and the image is interpreted! Indeed, the minds of people who read a thousand words or more per minute are able to handle 10 or 12 words at a time!

How do your emotions function when you read?

As was said earlier, it is not the intention of this book to delve into the psychiatric mysteries that make poor readers out of people who have all the physical equipment to become superior ones. I leave that problem to the men and women who are professionally qualified to treat such cases.

However, your reading efficiency can be affected by your emotional state from one time to the next. If you have had a quarrelsome day at home or on the job, you are not likely to be able to concentrate very well on a book or magazine. A balmy spring day may make it difficult for you to keep your attention fixed on an assigned piece of reading. You will recall that thoughts of a forthcoming vacation caused a sharp drop in achievement among students in a college reading course.

It is extremely important for you to remind yourself periodically that reading is more than a physical and mental process. When you wonder why the interest that prompted you to read this book is no longer there, look to your emotions. When you can't put your finger on what is responsible for your failure to make more progress in your practice sessions, look to your emotions. And when you feel like dropping the whole idea of improving your reading ability, get hold of your emotions.

Your emotions can influence how your mind interprets what you are reading. If you don't like the point of view of a writer of a particular piece, you may block out his ideas, however sensible they may be. Have you ever said, "_____ doesn't know what he (she) is talking about," simply because you didn't agree? You may decide, in advance, that certain material is too deep for you. Obviously, such an attitude will guarantee lack of understanding. You must try to control your emotions so that they do not interfere with either speed or comprehension. The person who boos a speaker rarely takes the trouble to listen.

The preceding explanation of how the reading mechanism works should have helped you realize that it is not too complicated for you to learn how to operate it efficiently. Approach the work ahead with confidence, care, and understanding. You will be delighted with the results.

How can you begin to improve your reading mechanism?

Your first job is to train yourself to increase the size of the images your eyes send to your mind. It is here that your *peripheral vision* assumes its most significant role. The ability of your eyes to see beyond their immediate focus is the major factor in eliminating word-by-word reading and controlling *subvocalization*.

The number of words a reader habitually identifies *during a particular pause* is known as the RECOGNITION SPAN. Thus, if your eyes stop only three times in reading a 12-word line, each recognition span can accommodate 2 to 5 words, depending upon the length of the individual words. Here are some general principles to bear in mind:

- The actual eye stops occur somewhere between the limits of the recognition span, sometimes on a word and at other times on the space between words. Material on both sides of the stop is absorbed.

- The eyes have a tendency to cover more words or letters to the right of a given stop than to the left. Thus the stop usually does not occur at midpoint in the recognition span but is overbalanced to the left.

- Since every reader gradually develops a basic rhythm in his eye movements, the stops assume a more or less uniform pattern across the lines. For the purposes of illustration, we will show the recognition spans in a uniform pattern, although you must understand that *it may not necessarily fit yours*. You will doubtless have to make adjustments as you practice, but that will be as it should be. It is impossible for anyone to predict how your eyes will behave. No two readers function exactly alike.

- As you will see in the examples below, there is not too great a difference in the recognition spans between the average and fast readers. It amounts to little more than a reduction of one or two stops per line.

In the following passages, the slanted lines, in one case, and the arrows in the others indicate the approximate widths of the recognition spans of the types of readers illustrated. Remember: the stops occur somewhere between the recognition spans, shading to the left.

Word-by-Word Reader

There / is / no / telling / how / many / different / "local / times" / there / were / in / the / United / States / prior / to / the / adoption / of / Standard / Time, / but / we / do / know / that / before / 1883 / there / were / something / like / 100 / different / times / in / use / by / the / railroads / of / this / country. /

Average Reader

⟨————⟩ ⟨————————⟩ ⟨————————⟩ ⟨————⟩
A traveler going from Maine to California, if anxious
⟨————⟩ ⟨————————————⟩ ⟨————⟩ ⟨————⟩
to have correct railroad time, was obliged to change his
⟨———⟩ ⟨———————————⟩
watch some twenty times during the journey.
⟨————————————⟩ ⟨————⟩ ⟨————⟩
In the railroad station in Buffalo, there were three
⟨———⟩ ⟨————————————⟩ ⟨————⟩
clocks—one set to New York time, one set to Columbus
⟨———⟩ ⟨————⟩ ⟨————⟩ ⟨————⟩
time, and the other set to local Buffalo time.

Fast Reader

⟨————————————————⟩ ⟨————————————————⟩
In Kansas City each of the leading jewelers furnished
⟨————————————————⟩ ⟨————————⟩
his own "standard time" and no two agreed. Sometimes the
⟨————————————————⟩ ⟨————————⟩
difference was as great as twenty minutes. Each jeweler
⟨————————————⟩ ⟨————————————⟩
took his own readings. He had his own customers who set

their watches by his regulator and were willing to wager on the correctness of his time.

The situation became so notorious that an astronomer was hired to untangle the mess. On his recommendation the problem was solved by the city's adoption of a "time ball" system.

Super-Speed Reader

These time balls, now almost forgotten, were a great institution in their time. Each day at official noon at a particular location, a large ball, sometimes three or four feet in diameter, so as to be visible for several miles, was dropped from a lofty mast. As the ball fell, the people—watching from many vantage points—set their timepieces at noon, and thus everyone in the city was provided with uniform time.

Did you notice that the word-by-word reader has more than twice as many stops as the average reader? One can manage no better than about 125 words a minute, whereas the other can proceed at a speed of 300-350 words a minute. You noticed, too, that the fast reader averages about two stops per line. No definite stop pattern can be established for the super-speed readers since some of these extraordinary people *can read right down a page,* making indeterminate stops only here or there, absorbing entire paragraphs in one sweep! If you can learn to do this some day, you will be in the top minute fraction of all readers.

*   *   *

We can now begin your training program for increasing your recognition span. You probably have, whether you realize it or not, considerable experience in this area. Note the following:

seven o'clock   across the street

NO TURN ON RED   The United States of America

I'm Dreaming of a White Christmas

In the split second it took your eyes to glance at each of the word groups above, your mind promptly recognized a familiar image: time, place, traffic sign, your country's full name, a popular seasonal song. The span went from two words to six, yet your reaction very likely was instantaneous regardless of the length. You absorbed the basic sense of each expression and were not even conscious of the number of words each had.

Even if you are a slow reader, there are thousands of other word groups that you recognize instantly without examining their piece-by-piece construction. The meaning of the familiar word-combinations comes in a flash because you have seen them before. Under such circumstances, your recognition span automatically increases to 3, 4, 5, or more words. All this means that your recognition span is acceptable sometimes. To become a skillful reader, you must train yourself to include *multiple word-groups in your eye stops every time*—whether you are familiar with them or not!

There is something else. Not only is it faster to read a word-group in one gulp, so to speak; it is also better for your understanding. The word-by-word reader becomes confused with phrases like *beginning of the end* or *early in the evening. Beginning-end, early-evening* seem contradictory when taken out of the context of their word-groups. The mind doesn't grasp the total image; it fails "to see the forest for the trees." We will have more to say about this problem in Chapter VII.

One more point. What you now know about the disadvantages of reading word-by-word should make doubly clear to you why *roadblocks* must be eliminated. If you point, mumble to yourself, move your head unnecessarily, or silently form words with your lips, you are forcing your recognition span to limit itself to single words at a glance. By taking advantage of your *peripheral vision* and cutting down on *subvocalization,* you make improvement possible. How harmful all obstacles to efficient reading are, how much they influence speed and comprehension, cannot be repeated too often.

EXERCISES

Your objective here is to use your peripheral vision to train yourself to see and understand ever larger groups of words at a glance. You must learn to concentrate on total images, not isolated words, thereby reducing subvocalization at the same time. Do not attempt to cover all the suggested exercises in one sitting. Our eventual schedule (Chapter X) will call for no more than 3 minutes a day of practicing the span-stretching skills, once you understand how to handle the drills. There will be enough variety for you to work with a different type each session. Be thorough, but be patient. You may not be very successful at first. Remind yourself that you are breaking some old, bad habits and trying to form new, better ones. It takes time and perseverance! Stay with it! You will gradually discover, as with the roadblocks, that certain exercises do you more good than others. When you have decided on your favorites, eliminate the ones that don't seem to work for you.

A. Flash Cards

Here we have one of the oldest training procedures in reading improvement programs. Similar drills are provided in clinics by machines (tachistoscopes) that flash word-groups on screens for fractions of seconds. For home study purposes, the flash cards can be quite effective, too, if you carefully follow the instructions for each type of exercise.

You will need a supply of 3″ by 5″ index cards and a great deal of dogged determination to do the work involved. From any reading source, including the various exercises scattered throughout this book, select random word-groups. In the sample list that follows, note that the phrases contain 3–5 words. If later you want to set up drills with larger word-groups, do not do so until you feel comfortable reading with 3 or fewer stops per line. When you think you can "graduate" to try 2 stops per line regularly, you can prepare flash cards containing 5–7 words in each phrase.

Sample List of Random Phrases

a flight of bombers	totally wiped out
none of the boys	down the garden path
almost equally exciting	several days later
many of the pilgrims	put into gear
the rest of them	thrown out at home
the light fantastic	wall to wall carpeting
eluded the police	for sentimental reasons
mowed the grass	totally different ideas
quickly disposed of	slowly but surely
in a passionate embrace	a remarkable job
the British Parliament	a feeling of guilt
first fall planting	behind the rocks

in an hour or so
The United States of America
toys, books, and crayons
result of a survey
Taming of the Shrew
by word of mouth
the thousands cheered
first on the program
plan of attack
behind the window
down the middle
plunged into the water
lifted the package
superior reading skill
to many home owners
clearly and distinctly
developing better habits
master the techniques
Girl of the Golden West
from Spain to Portugal
be equally harmful
chop down the tree
for the majority
busy daily schedule
half the battle
spoke rather rapidly
too little knowledge
not too early, Joe
roast turkey and gravy
at the end of the month
on the front cover
a transcontinental journey
and you, too, Tom
four years at college
no, of course not
rather seriously hurt

a flight of bees
with great force
who had voted
seven league boots
sworn to secrecy
gales of laughter
lazy days of summer
with Joe and Bill
a restful night
a roar of delight
not for very long
by the running brook
far away and long ago
tall, dark, and handsome
with a loud shout
The Star-Spangled Banner
in your back yard
a thousand times *No*
that deadly routine
to send it home
as a matter of fact
has been written
amount of instruction
panes of glass
trying to learn
prepared to accept
handful of peanuts
home medical adviser
long since disappeared
far from the crowd
a very flat tire
with reasonable pride
slippery as an eel
under clean sheets
not to be believed
Oh, my aching back

split down the middle   a first class effort
a mass of stuff   right over the counter

Flash Card Drill 1

Preparation: Type or print a different phrase on each of
40 cards, centering the material thus:

```
on a Sunday morning
```

Instructions: Collect the cards into a pack, faces down,
so that when you lift a card the words will be right side
up. Now lift a card, facing it up just long enough to grasp
the phrase as it flashes before your eyes. *Do not read the
phrase aloud! Try not to say it in your mind!* You want to
avoid vocalizing or subvocalizing. Let the image register
and move on. After each flash-look, immediately place the
card face down in front of the pack. Continue to lift and
drop each card until you have finished the pack.

How will you know you caught a phrase before you
put the card down? I can say this categorically: *you will
know!* Your mind will either accept the image or signal
to you that you missed it. Trust your eyes and mind.

At the beginning of this drill, use whatever speed is
comfortable for you in the lift-and-drop procedure. With
practice, you will be able to decrease the time needed to
expose the phrase for the flash-look. You will develop

speed flexibility, just as is possible with the machine (tachistoscope) we mentioned.

Prepare three or four packs. Use them alternately about a half dozen times or until you have become too familiar with the word-groups. Then set up new packs of cards by copying some of the numerous phrases you will find in the exercises that follow. When you can go through a pack of cards as fast as you can lift-and-drop them, you will not need to do this drill more than once a month, and eventually not at all. If you can get someone to work the flash cards for you, so much the better.

Flash Card Drill 2

Preparation: On the next 24 cards, type or print the phrases centered at the bottom:

```
several years ago
```

Instructions: This technique is a variation of the one we have just presented. From the second pack of cards, select a dozen or so. Now place this book on a table, with the wide side facing you and the binding at the rear. Insert the cards at about 25-page intervals between the pages, with the phrases centered at the bottom of each card facing you. After you have inserted the cards, grasp the book with your thumb under the bottom cover and your remaining four fingers on the top cover. Using your thumb to flip the pages, do so until you come to the first phrase card and go slightly past it. Here again, the idea is to absorb the word-group within a single recognition span in the split second it is visible before it is covered by the pages. Continue flipping pages until you have identified all the cards, and then replace them with others. *Reminder: no vocalization, no subvocalization!* When you become skilled in the method of using flash cards, you will be doing with the pages of a book what is done in reading laboratories with very expensive equipment. Again, prepare additional packs of cards as soon as the phrases become too familiar.

Flash Card Drill 3

Preparation: On the next 36 cards, type or print the random phrases centered at the extreme left of each card:

```
too far to walk
```

Instructions: Place the pack of cards, faces up, on the table. Cover the first phrase with a blank card. Insert more blanks alternately so that each phrase card is covered by a blank. Grasp the pack with both hands, thumbs resting on top and other fingers underneath. Bend the pack down and, as you release the bend, lift your right thumb slightly and press down gently with the left. Do this several times until the cards have been spread to the left well enough to be flipped individually. If you have ever tried to count tickets, you will understand how to spread the cards.

Now, flip the first blank card, exposing the first phrase for a split second before you flip the next blank card to cover it. Continue until you have finished the pack. Again, *no vocalization, no subvocalization!* Just let each phrase register in your mind. Prepare additional packs as the phrases become overly familiar.

B. Span-Stretching Exercises in Columns

Several exercises will now be presented with the contents broken up into word-groups and arranged in vertical columns. Your objective will be to follow the sense of the paragraphs as *your eyes move down the page and absorb the individual phrases in single stops.* You must try to hold your head and eyes fixed—no lateral movements—as you sweep down the page. This will not be easy, but persistent practice will make it possible.

COLUMN EXERCISE 1

Spills Thrill!

```
D                                                    D
O    Water skiing has become                         O
W    America's fastest growing water sport.          W
N    Exceedingly easy to learn                        N
     water skiing is one of
     the few "one lesson" sports.
     You can learn the basics
     of the "take-off"
     on dry land,
     then transfer the knowledge
     to a deep water start—
     which you make from
     a sitting position in water
     which reaches your shoulders.
     As the tow boat
```

gradually increases speed,
you rise slowly
until you are standing
with back straight
and knees slightly bent.
You are now skimming
along the water's surface
at about 20 miles per hour.
You take the turns
on the outside
so as not to slacken
the ski rope;
you bend your knees
to absorb the slight shock
of passing across
the boat's wake—
you gather confidence, even daring
and raise one arm
to wave toward the shore.
By the end of a long weekend
you may have ventured
a few tricks—
and had a few spills.

COMPREHENSION TEST

Another title for this selection could be:

    a. Elbows, arms, and legs
    b. Fast speedboats
    c. Water tricks
    d. A popular water sport

ANSWER: The fourth letter in the alphabet.

COLUMN EXERCISE 2

Here you will find somewhat larger word-groups (some containing as many as 7 words). Do not try it until you feel comfortable with the 3–5 words phrases. Continue as before—*one glance per line, one stop, one word-group, no head movements laterally,* and *no subvocalization.* Go faster than you think you should. Again, there will be a comprehension test at the end.

But Can You Stay in Love?

BY SYDNEY J. HARRIS

D
O
W
N

Being in love (or thinking you are
which amounts to the same thing)
when you are young is
an exhilarating experience but
it is also easy and commonplace.
I was in love half-a-hundred times
during my adolescence.
There is no trick to it.
A pretty face, a turned-up nose,
a fetching figure is
often all it takes.
Sometimes even less than that—
sometimes just a glimpse of
a golden girl turning a corner
in the dusk and you know
it is She, The One.
Being in love is a natural
and inevitable state of youth.
In those years we are
only half-alive when we
are out of love.
We live in a condition

D
O
W
N

67

of perpetual self-delusion
intoxicated with our dreams.
But to be older and in love—
to be in love for a long time—
to be in love
as middle age approaches,
and responsibilities bear down,
and vexations crop up—
this is worthy of celebration
in song and story.
Love is worth nothing
until it passes through
the fever of infatuation,
until it settles down to a
steady day-by-day routine,
until the golden girl begins
to fade around the edges,
and the lithe, lean boy
begins to fatten in the middle.
Anybody can be young and in love;
it is hard *not* to be.
But only those graced by the gods
can persist in loving
when the chill of autumn
begins to set in.
For love is an act of will,
not a sentiment;
it may start in the blood,
but it can only be sustained
by the mind and the spirit.

COMPREHENSION TEST

Another title for this selection could be:

    a. Boy and girl
    b. Young people in love

    c. Lasting love
    d. Lost love

ANSWER: The third letter of the alphabet.

To set up additional exercises of phrases arranged in columns, try this device. Get two pieces of stiff plastic or cardboard, 1½″ high and 3″ wide. On one piece, mark off a slot *centered on the left* 1¾″ wide by ³⁄₁₆″ high and draw the lines thus:

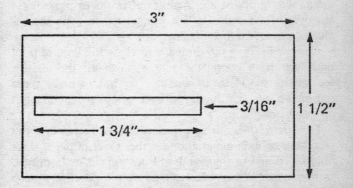

On the other piece, mark off a slot *centered left* 2″ wide by ³⁄₁₆″ high and draw the lines. Using a razor blade or a sharp knife, cut out the slots along the drawn lines, leaving a narrow opening in each card. You now have what we can call a *phrase-marker*. The 1¾″ slot will cover half a line of print in a paperback. The 2″ slot will cover half a line of print in a full-sized book, or a full line of print in most newspaper columns or digest magazines in which articles are printed in two-column pages.

After you have constructed your *phrase-makers,* select a brief passage, about 150–250 words, from any type of reading source just mentioned. Using the appropriate card, place the slotted opening at the left of the first line of print. *Throughout this preparation of column drills, make no attempt to read the selection as you normally would.* Concentrate only on the word-phrases revealed by the slot.

If you have located the card properly, you will see half a line of print. At the top of a sheet of paper, jot down as much of the phrase as you think you can handle. Then slide the slot to the right to reveal the rest of the line and jot down the next phrase. Limit yourself to no more than two or three phrases per line, certainly only two if you are aiming at 500 wpm. If pieces of words or phrases are left over at the end of a line, combine them with the beginning phrase on the next line.

Continue sliding the slotted card along the lines of print until you have completed jotting down all the phrases located by the slots. Remember: try not to make sense out of the selection until you have completed breaking it up into word-groups.

For best results during practice, it is suggested that you type your column material on another sheet of paper since phrases copied in longhand will not approximate printed word-groups. When you are ready for a practice session with any one of your newly created column drills from your growing collection, reread the directions for reading down a column for speed and understanding. Incidentally, you can use your self-constructed column drills to build up additional packs of flash cards.

When you have become confident enough in your training to go beyond 2 or 3 stops per line, you can use the 2″ slotted card to practice reading full lines of print in single stops in newspapers or digest magazines. Simply start with the slot at the first line and *slide the card downward as you read. WARNING:* The slotted card sliding down a column is useful practice for a time, but this technique should be discarded as soon as possible. Try to learn to read down a column without the card, which can become a new roadblock if it is over-used.

Typical Newspaper Column

Rodeo stars and football players have discovered that wearing women's panty girdles gives them added protection against torn muscles. Because of its grip, a knee-length panty girdle can prevent the thighs from splitting when a rider lands on the back of a bucking bull, steer, or horse, reports *Medical World News*. The girdle prevents all kinds of bruises, tears, and ruptures that might be caused by the rider's abruptly hitting the animal's sharp spine. And football players with sore hamstrings have found that wearing a girdle can prevent further injury to those muscles.

C. Rhythm Exercises

The flash card and column drills are useful in training your eyes to increase the number of words they can handle at a glance. However, merely stretching your recognition span with isolated phrases is only preliminary. You must be able to transfer your new skill to regular lines of print in books. To become a rapid reader, you will have to learn to make fewer than three stops per line, consistently absorbing 4–7 words during each stop. The exercises that follow are designed to help you develop a rhythm in your eye movements appropriate to your goals. Your practice sessions should move you gradually from a three-stop-per-line pattern to a two-stop sweep—perhaps some day to even faster rhythms.

So that the exercises will approximate what you actually do when you read, comprehension questions will be added to some of the drills. There would be no point, certainly, in practicing mechanical stretching of the word-span without introducing the most important element—understanding.

Rhythm Drill 1

In the first set, we will start modestly, three stops per line. You will notice that a series of dots (points of eye stops) have been placed on lines (limits of recognition spans). Focus on the dot and use your peripheral vision to absorb the limits of the line at either end. Then let your eyes slide to the next dot, and finally to the last on the line. Make your return sweep and proceed wtih the next series of dots and lines.

In the second set, random phrases will be introduced among the dots and lines to illustrate the actual size the recognition spans might take in a three-stop-per-line speed. The third set will present a sample paragraph, with the dots indicating where a reader's stop might occur over the word-groups. Your eyes will presumably absorb material both to the left and right of each dot, forming phrases of 3–5 words.

The purpose of the 3-step exercise is to set likely or typical patterns for your eyes so that the conscious effort to make a given number of stops per line will develop into a consistent rhythm. Of course, the dots and lines are arbitrarily arranged; your own stops and recognition spans on lines of print will vary with the material being read.

Increase your speed gradually. Stay with one rhythmic pattern until you are so comfortable with it that you feel ready to move on to the wider spans represented by exercises (b) and (c). Do not allow yourself to become confused by practicing more than one 3-step exercise during any single session.

a. Rhythm Pattern

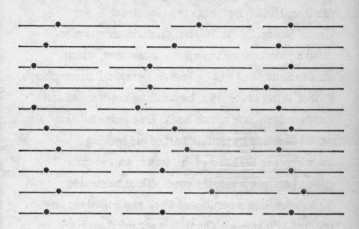

b. Random Phrases

—•———— in an abandoned building ——•———
——•———— ——•———— with enormous energy
a part of the process ——•———— ——•————
——•———— ——— all kinds of things ——•——
——•——— ——•———— On a yellow bicycle
a quick change artist ——•———— ——•————
——•———————— good times at the beach —•——
—•—— ——•———— about three miles north
different point of view ——•———— ——•————
————•———— unsafe at any speed ——————

c. Sample Paragraph

In the flick of an eye it takes you to read
this line, 16,000 matches are being struck in the
United States. Of the 500 billion matches manufactured a year, 200 billion are book matches, which
were invented in 1892 by Joshua Pusey, a Philadelphia
lawyer. After many tries, he made an economical and
comparatively safe match book. He eliminated acci-
dental flare-ups by putting part of the igniting
ingredients in the head of the match, part in the
striking surface inside the cover. Then he stapled
50 matches into a cardboard book and called his new
product "Flexibles." The public regarded his book
matches as dangerous because sparks from a lighted
match often ignited others. Finally, the match
company, which had bought his invention, put the
striking surface outside the book and printed "Close
cover before striking" on the flap. From then on
book matches began to be ordered in the millions.

COMPREHENSION TEST

Write *T* (True) or *F* (False) in the space provided
before each statement:

_____ Book matches are manufactured in the billions.
_____ Joshua Pusey was successful in his first try.

_____ The public regarded the early book matches as dangerous.

_____ The safety problem has never been solved.

ANSWERS: T, F, T, F.

Rhythm Drill 2

In this exercise, we will vary 3-stop lines with 2-stop lines, a rhythm that should approximate 300-400 wpm. Reminder: *no subvocalization* when you practice with the random phrases and sample pararaphs.

a. Rhythm Pattern

b. Random Phrases

—————•————————— an unusual outdoor art show
————•————————— for the first time ————•—————
to see an interesting movie ————————•—————

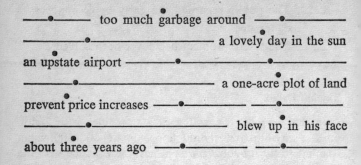

———•——— too much garbage around ———•———————

——————————•—————————————— a lovely day in the sun

an upstate airport ———————•————————— •————————

——————————•————————————— a one-acre plot of land

prevent price increases ————•———— ————•————

——————————•———————————— blew up in his face

about three years ago ————•———— ————•————

c. Sample Paragraphs

Paper matches are tested as they come from the machine. You can try a test. If the match goes out in one breath, it is too easily extinguished, and would be useless outdoors. If it takes three puffs, it is dangerous, for it is likely to be thrown away while lighted. Two quick puffs are just right for ordinary breezes and are called safe.

Book matches have been used to advertise everything from chewing gum to the need for an apartment during World War II. General MacArthur dropped four million packages bearing the prophecy "I Shall Return" over the Philippines. Political candidates use them. The White House has them for the Presidents. Thousands of Americans save book matches as a hobby. A man in Fort Worth is said to have the largest collection—over 50,000.

COMPREHENSION TEST

Again *T* or *F* in the spaces provided:

_____ Paper matches are tested periodically.

_____ The safest require two puffs to blow out.

_____ Advertising on book matches is quite rare.

_____ Book matches have been dropped from planes as propaganda.

_____ Some people save book matches as a hobby.

ANSWERS: T, T, F, T, T

Rhythm Drill 3

Do not try this exercise until you think you can read at a 2-stop-per-line pace (about 500 wpm). When you reach the super-speed class, you will read right down the page and will not need preliminary rhythm drills or dot-and-line exercises.

a. Rhythm Pattern

b. Random Phrases

for at least two weeks ————————•————————

————————•———————— a call to the local police

a series of loud explosions ————————•————————

————————•———————— at the scene of the accident

customers fleeing from the store ————————•————————

————————•———————— long lines at the gas pumps

set up to teach rural women ————————•————————

————————•———————— one of the top men in his field

could not be determined at once ————————•————————

————————•———————— the economic impact of the strike

c. Sample Paragraph

A bowler may be big or little, skinny or fat,
young or old, man or woman. Three-year-olds, the
blind, and people in wheel chairs are among the millions who roll the "big black apple" each year and
enjoy the satisfying sound of the ball crashing down
the pins. Bowling is a game that doesn't demand all-
out proficiency in order to enjoy it. No opponent
can frustrate your best shots, and an occasional
bowler can add up a higher score than an expert. But
it's far from being all luck. Skill puts the ball
where it will down the ten pins regularly. Sometimes,
though, luck combines with skill.

COMPREHENSION TEST

Again, *T* (True) and *F* (False) in the spaces:

_____ Only the young and strong can bowl.

_____ You have to be good to enjoy the game.

_____ Luck can lead to a very high score.

_____ In the long run, skill will tell.

ANSWERS: F, F, T, T

Practice Paragraphs (Bowling article continued)

For instance, no one has duplicated the feat of an unknown bowler who had rolled a series of perfect frames and delivered his last ball for a strike. But one of the pins split in half lengthwise, and one half bounded back and stood up in about its original spot. That's the only case where a bowler bowled 299½ out of 300.

Records state that bowling started as a religious ceremony in Europe about 300 A.D. Peasants carried clubs for defense even to confession. To dramatize religion, priests had the peasants stand their clubs in a corner and roll large stones at the clubs which stood for sins. A club knocked down was a sin overcome, one left standing was a sin to be conquered. *Nine pins,* brought over here by the Dutch, became so popular in the early days that the authorities banned it to prevent gambling. The law definitely stated

"nine" pins. A little later on someone added another
pin and the game became *ten pins,* with no law to prevent its enjoyment. By 1900, the American Bowling
Congress had started bowling on its way to an Olympic
sport. An opposing bowling team at the 1936 Olympics
wondered how the Americans could roll a hook ball unless their ball was other than the regulation one.
The ABC soon convinced them it was the Americans'
skill, for the congress had devised a scale to weigh
one quarter of the ball at a time and thus guard
against any attempt to use a "loaded" bowling ball.

COMPREHENSION TEST

T (True), *F* (False) in the spaces:

_____ A bowler once counted a half pin in his score.
_____ Clubs and sins were part of the origin of bowling.
_____ The Dutch declared *ten pins* illegal.
_____ The Americans introduced the hook ball at the
Olympics.

ANSWERS: T, T, F, T

D. Center-Line Exercises

You are probably familiar with a popular audience-
participation session called a "sing-along." An organist,
band or choral leader has the lyrics of a song flashed on
a screen line by line. A bouncing ball hovers over the
words to help the audience keep time with the music and
identify the phrase in sequence as the mass singing pro-
ceeds.

When you are beginning to feel fairly comfortable with

the two-stop-per-line reading pace, you can borrow the idea of the "sing-along" to develop another device for setting up practice sessions. Use a paperback—and later a full-sized book—that you own and are willing to mark up. Draw a light penciled line down the center of each of the first six pages. Omit the line on the next six pages.

Have a stopwatch or a watch with a second hand available. You are to time yourself as you do this exercise. Keep in mind that you will make one stop to the left of the vertical marker on each line and another stop to the right. Take note of the time as you begin to read. *Imagine a bouncing ball pausing once to the left of the marker and then swinging over to pause again to the right.* Keep on reading as your eyes follow the imaginary bouncing ball hovering over the word-groups! After you have completed the first six marked pages, read the next six without trying to be conscious of an imaginary bouncing ball.

If you can eventually read both the marked and unmarked twelve pages in a total of eight minutes or less, you will have attained a reading speed of more than 500 *wpm*. It will take time for you to perfect this technique, but it is worth the effort. Many of my students have told me that one major advantage of "following the bouncing ball" is that it helps to cut down subvocalization.

* * *

You now have your choice of four types of exercises to "stretch your span": flash cards, column drills, dot-and-line patterns, and center-line read-alongs. Let your preference and need for variety determine which one(s) you use during any practice session. It should be stressed that all of the suggested techniques have, at best, an artificial quality about them in comparison to the smooth, unselfconscious reading habits you wish to perfect. Your goal, therefore, should be to discard the drills as soon as you think you can get along without them. People learning new dance steps stop counting after the proper routines have been established. You, too, must strive to reach a stage in your rate improvement program where you do not direct your eye movements mechanically but allow them to respond effortlessly to a trained speed pattern suited to the type of material being read.

CHAPTER VII

STEP THREE:

Look for the Keys!

ALL RIGHT.

Let's take stock.

What have you learned so far?

About Reading Improvement Generally

1. By practicing faithfully, *you can help yourself* improve your reading ability.

2. You get best results from short practice sessions on a daily basis.

3. To retain your new skills, you should apply them frequently in normal reading situations.

About Reading Rate

1. You must eliminate all self-imposed obstacles to rapid reading.

2. When you read faster, you normally understand better, provided the contents, your purpose, and attempted speed are properly coordinated.

3. You need not look at every letter of every word to absorb the sense of a group of words.

4. Reading words in groups is essential to improving rate and comprehension.

5. The difficulty of a selection should determine your rate. You should not try to read all material at the same speed.

Our summary reveals that the emphasis up to this point has been on speed. However, following most practice selections you were given a test in comprehension. There was good reason for this, as you were repeatedly told. Unless faster reading is accompanied by better understanding, you derive little benefit from your training program. Progress in rate and comprehension cannot be separated. Each is very much dependent on the other. Admittedly we treat these two abilities in separate chapters. But we do so because we are attempting to break down the basic reading skills and fit them into our 5-Step Plan.

Now, as we shift the emphasis to comprehension, you must not assume that we are finished with rate. In reality, we are approaching it from another direction. Improvement in comprehension will inevitably lead to a faster rate.

A reading authority recently said:

"A special fire is kindled when the reader and writer meet."

This is a beautiful description of the remarkable thing that happens after one person puts words on paper and another is thus enabled to obtain an intimate glimpse into the operation of a human mind. Of course, no one can expect to uncover the complete picture of the mental processes and emotional reactions that went into the writing. But the "special fire" surely burns brighter when the writer has found the best possible words and the reader brings to them his maximum appreciation and understanding.

There are many sides to the problem of comprehension. One of the difficulties is that your degree of understanding of a given passage cannot be measured as exactly as can your speed of reading it. Your rate can be timed and we can express your results in terms of words-per-minute. But even if we ask a few content questions after you have read a selection and you answer them all correctly, have we really proved that you and the writer had a mutual exchange? Besides knowing *what* he said, have you understood *why* he wrote what he did? Were you able to draw conclusions from *what he left out* as well as from *what he put in?* Did he seem to be looking down his nose at you, or was he warm and friendly? Did you believe what he said because he proved it, because he is a well-known expert—or did you wonder whether he had a special ax to grind and was distorting the facts to suit his purpose? In short, did you try to match your own experience, background, and information with the author's; did the words mean the same to you when you read them as they did to him when he wrote them?

In connection with the last remark, I am reminded of the time a certain play opened in New York and was greeted with great respect by all the critics. Each one quarreled with the others about the theme. The audience, too, was split into two camps—those who were sure they had read the dramatist's message correctly and those who walked out utterly confused. Finally, the author himself was invited to comment on the storm of interpretations that had been stirred up here. His reply went something like this: *I am delighted to find so many things in my play that I didn't realize I had put in.*

I offer the story to suggest that it is possible to disagree on what a writer is trying to say. Usually, however, the meaning is perfectly plain and readily ascertained *if you know what to look for.* An author uses key words and sentences to project his ideas, attitudes, and beliefs. Your job is to find these keys so that you will be able not only to understand what he said but also to answer some of the questions that go beyond the bare facts. It would be easy to give you a set of exercises and ask you to get the main ideas, remember a few of the details, and make an effort to evaluate some of the other features that can be found in any piece of writing. But you already know that this is the way you should be reading. Your problem is mainly *how* this is done.

If you wanted to become an expert appraiser of fine furniture, you would not go to a completed cabinet for your training. You would very likely start with a study of wood grains and textures; proceed to learn how various joints are made and fastened with nails, screws, and glue; and finally become familiar with finishes. It is always a good idea to study construction before attempting to evaluate the finished product.

So it is with reading. Improving your comprehension must start with a study of how a piece of writing begins and how it develops. In this way you can learn to recognize the structural elements of reading matter and thus can easily find the keys inserted by the author to assist your understanding.

The tool of all writing is the sentence. It is the basic means of expressing a single thought or, in combination, developing an idea. Even the poet, who takes great liberties with the language, doesn't ignore this fundamental law of communication. Observe the following:

a) I never saw a moor, I never saw the sea; yet know I how the heather looks, and what a wave must be.

b) I never saw a moor,
   I never saw the sea;
   Yet know I how the heather looks,
   And what a wave must be.

One way (prose) or the other (the way the poet, Emily Dickinson, actually wrote it), the writer must tell us what he/she is talking about and then say something about it.

A young child uses a sentence to express practically everything that is on his mind. He says, "I want a toy." There is nothing more to be said. He has identified an object, has expressed a desire for it, and that's that. There would be no purpose in trying to look behind or ahead of the statement. The child isn't old enough to have developed shades of meaning, subtlety, or cleverly concealed emotions.

An adult rarely confines himself to single sentences. He uses them in combination because his greater maturity prompts him to be more specific, give more details, explain the *whys* and *hows* of his remarks. In fact, we become suspicious when a grownup stops at one sentence. If a guest in your house got up suddenly, grumbled, "I'm going home," and left without another word, you would be sure that something had been said or done to offend him. In his case the sentence would not have revealed everything that was on his mind when he expressed himself. His emotions, his state of health, even the quality of his judgment, might all have become subjects of discussion after he left.

When we have progressed, therefore, from the primary levels of language use, we tend to speak and write in paragraphs. And yet, if we examine one of these, we must

conclude that it is an expanded version of a basic sentence.
Note:

a) A walk in the rain is not for me.

> What are we talking about?
> *A walk in the rain . . .*
>
> What have we said about it?
> *. . . is not for me.*

b) A walk in the rain is not for me. I can't imagine
why anyone would prefer soggy shoes, wet socks, and
clammy clothing to a big, soft arm chair, a crackling fire,
and a puzzling detective story. Who wouldn't trade a
spattered nose and tightly closed lips for a mouth munch-
ing contentedly on peanuts and chocolate bars? I'm not a
duck, I don't believe jackets are water repellent, and I'd
rather take a shower without my clothes on. Sloshing
about in puddles is for traffic cops and night watchmen. I
like to do my walking on a rainy day when I can wiggle
my bare toes in a thick, plush carpet!

> What does the first sentence establish?
> *The main idea of the paragraph*
>
> What do the other sentences contribute?
> *Clarification of the main idea*

Of course, the additional sentences in a paragraph
enable a writer to insert details, emotion, color, and
sound. But the reader comes away with the same basic
idea supplied by the key sentence. The latter is called the
topic sentence; it announces what will be discussed. Several *supporting sentences* enrich the initial thought and
expand it into a coherent idea. A *concluding sentence,*

usually but not always present, gives both a summary and a lead into other ideas the writer might want to pursue. In general, the basic structure of the paragraph holds true regardless of the nature of the material:

From a magazine article written by a naturalist:

Next night, as I stood in the moonlight, I saw skunks dancing. There were seven of them, probably a family, and they formed a circle in the forest glade. They moved in rhythmic jumps until they were nose-to-nose. Then, with tails waving like fan dancers' plumes, they hopped backward to the circle's edge, then shuffle-jumped forward again. Observers have been unable to read anything into this dance except good nature and social playfulness. I'm happy with that definition.

From "Kon-Tiki," a nonfiction adventure story by Thor Heyerdahl:

But the men knew little about rafts. A raft—that wasn't a ship; it had no keel or bulwarks. It was just something floating on which to save oneself in an emergency, until one was picked up by a boat of some kind. One of the men, nevertheless, had great respect for rafts in the open sea; he had drifted about on one for three weeks when a German torpedo sank his ship in mid-Atlantic.

"But you can't navigate a raft," he added. "It goes sideways and backward and round as the wind takes it."

From "The Call of the Wild," a novel by Jack London:

Buck's first day on the Dyea beach was like a nightmare. Every hour was filled with shock and surprise. He had been suddenly jerked from the heart of civilization and flung into the heart of things primordial. No lazy, sun-kissed life was this, with nothing to do but loaf and be bored. Here was neither peace, nor rest, nor a moment of safety. All was confusion and action, and every moment life and limb were in peril. There was imperative need to be constantly alert, for these dogs and men were not town dogs and men. They were savages, all of them, who knew no law but the law of club and fang.

In each of the sample paragraphs, the main idea has been established by the end of the first sentence, and the rest of the sentences supply details and the finishing touch. Certainly not all paragraphs have a set length, nor do they invariably begin with a topic sentence and end with a concluding one. For instance, in the following brief paragraph from Joseph Hilton's "Lost Horizon," the structural pattern is literally reversed:

They were still conversing when a sharp but brief ascent robbed them of breath, inducing in a few paces all their earlier strain. Presently the ground leveled, and they stepped out of the mist into clear, sunny air. Ahead, and only a short distance away, lay the lamasery of Shangri-La.

As you see, there is great flexibility in paragraph construction, but every one is designed to center attention on a *single idea,* just as every sentence expresses a single thought. There may be more words in one than in another, but the end result is the same.

And this isn't all. If an author wishes to write more than a paragraph, he simply expands once more. A diagram of the process would look like this:

Paragraph	Article or Short Story	Book
Topic sentence	Introductory paragraph	Introductory chapter
Supporting sentences	Body paragraph(s)	Body chapters
Concluding sentence	Concluding paragraph	Concluding chapter

All writing, therefore, regardless of its length, points in a single direction. A book has a single major theme that is the conclusion of everything that has been said. Each chapter treats a single phase of the larger subject. Every paragraph in a chapter presents a single idea to support the main point. And the sentences in a paragraph produce the single thoughts that add up to the main idea.

*　　　*　　　*

I hope you have come along patiently with me to this point. The technical explanation of the writing process was necessary to reinforce my recommendation that knowing how an author writes helps you understand him better when you read. An author begins with the germ of an idea, works on it until he has decided the length and direction it will take, and then breaks it down into paragraphs or chapters to express his thoughts on the subject.

When you read, you literally reverse the process! If it is a single paragraph you are reading, you know that you can get into it and out of it quickly because you are looking for one idea. You will notice the details as you go along, but if you can't add them up to a main point, you have missed it. This gives you the *how* of reading. Look for the topic sentence, which announces what the paragraph will be about, note rapidly how it is developed, and then go on to the next one. No matter how much additional time you spend on a paragraph, you will still come out with one main idea, if it has been properly written.

If it is an article or book, you know *in advance of your reading* that there is going to be a main point the author is driving at, that his supporting ideas or plot manipulations (as in a novel) will be found *one by one* in the paragraphs or chapters, and that the quality of his work will be judged by the nature of his presentation of the details in the individual sentences. This knowledge of how to direct your mind can be of tremendous help to you. It supplies you with the tool that makes it possible for you to cut through masses of words, locate the important ideas, and move on with full speed and comprehension.

Here is another point about comprehension that should be clearer to you now. If a paragraph is an expanded sentence, word-by-word reading becomes a serious obstacle in the search for main ideas. Actually, if it were possible for most of us to read whole paragraphs within single recognition spans, that would be the best way to locate the single idea every paragraph develops. But most paragraphs are so long that only a very few of us should attempt to develop such a skill. However, there should be no question about the desirability of handling at least *groups of words* to avoid getting lost among the pieces and thereby missing the whole idea. A writer's details, comparisons, contrasts, examples, anecdotes, dialogue, and statistics are inserted to enable the reader to see the point of each paragraph clearly and thus move step by step in the direction of the basic theme or story of the selection as a whole.

And what about the other aspects of comprehension we mentioned before—the emotional tone of the material, its authoritative quality, the point of view, the charm and wit? Here, too, failure to concentrate on the whole, rather than its parts, prevents you from escaping the "tyranny of words." To test the quality of a suit, you wouldn't count the threads. All you need to remember a funny story is the punch line. The details come of themselves. If a speaker outlines a plan and you center your attention on his resonant voice and rich choice of words, you may not realize until it is too late that you are in no position to judge either the quality of the speech or its contents.

You must train your mind to attack every paragraph purposefully. Try to get the main idea quickly, form reactions along the way, and keep going steadily—all the while building up toward the general objective or theme the writer set out to develop. Rarely does missing a small detail or word here and there seriously interfere with your understanding of the important features of the material. You shouldn't clutter up your mind with the little things. Let it be free to concentrate on the big ideas.

Now let's try to apply some of the techniques we have been discussing to the opening three paragraphs of Washington Irving's "The Legend of Sleepy Hollow." I have selected this author because, although he wrote more than a hundred years ago, he can well serve as a model for any writer who wishes to present clear, correct, and interesting material. As you read, LOOK FOR THE KEYS! Decide what the paragraph is going to talk about, race through the details, and go on to the next. After you have finished your reading, there will be a test, the results of which will indicate to you what you should have been looking for. If you do well, you will know that you have uncovered the trade secret of rapid comprehension.

About two miles from the village of Tarrytown on the Hudson there is a little valley which is one of the quietest places in the whole world. It is known as Sleepy Hollow because a drowsy, dreamy influence seems to hang over the land and to pervade the very atmosphere. Its people are descendants of the original Dutch settlers, and are given to all kinds of marvelous beliefs. Strange tales are told of trances and visions and ghostly visitors. The apparition most frequently seen is that of a headless figure on horseback which is said by some to be the ghost of a Hessian trooper who rides forth nightly in quest of his head. The Headless Horseman of Sleepy Hollow is known far and wide in the Hudson Valley and is even said to have been seen by visitors as well as by the inhabitants of the dreamy village.

In this by-place of nature there abode, in a remote period of American history, that is to say some thirty years since, a worthy wight by the name of Ichabod Crane, who sojourned, or, as he expressed it, "tarried," in Sleepy Hollow, for the purpose of instructing the children of the vicinity. He was a native of Connecticut, a state which supplies the Union with pioneers of the mind as well as for the forest, and sends forth yearly its legions of frontier woodsmen and country schoolmasters. The cognomen of Crane was not inapplicable to his person. He was tall, and exceedingly lank, with narrow shoulders, long arms and legs, hands that dangled a mile out of his sleeves, feet that might have served for shovels, and his whole frame most loosely hung together. His head was small, and flat at top, with huge ears, large green glassy eyes, and a long snipe nose, so that it looked like a weathercock perched upon his spindle neck to tell which way the wind blew. To see him striding along the profile of a hill on a windy day, with his clothes bagging and fluttering about him, one might have mistaken him for the genius of famine descending upon the earth, or some scarecrow eloped from a cornfield.

His schoolhouse was a low building of one large

94

room, rudely constructed of logs; the windows partly glazed, and partly patched with leaves of old copybooks. It was most ingeniously secured at vacant hours, by a withe [twig] twisted in the handle of the door, and stakes set against the window shutters: so that though a thief might get in with perfect ease, he would find embarrassment in getting out—an idea most probably borrowed by the architect, Yost Van Houten, from the mystery of the eelpot. The schoolhouse stood in a rather lonely but pleasant situation, just at the foot of a woody hill, with a brook running close by, and a formidable birch tree growing at one end of it. From hence the low murmur of his pupils' voices, conning over their lessons, might be heard in a drowsy summer's day, like the hum of a beehive; interrupted now and then by the authoritative voice of the master, in the tone of menace or command; or, peradventure, by the appalling sound of the birch, as he urged some tardy loiterer along the flowery path of knowledge. Truth to say, he was a conscientious man, and ever bore in mind the golden maxim, "Spare the rod and spoil the child." Ichabod Crane's scholars certainly were not spoiled.

COMPREHENSION TEST

I. Main Ideas and Details

A. The over-all purpose of the author in the first three paragraphs was

_____ 1. to tell how cruel Crane was

_____ 2. to introduce the main character and setting of the story

_____ 3. to tell what school was like in the olden days

B. A title that could express the main idea of the first paragraph would be

_____ 1. A superstitious old town

_____ 2. A headless horseman

_____ 3. A Hessian trooper

C. A title for the second paragraph would be

_____ 1. A native of Connecticut

_____ 2. An eloped scarecrow

_____ 3. A funny-looking schoolteacher

D. A title for the third paragraph would be

_____ 1. Activities in an old schoolhouse

_____ 2. A stern teacher

_____ 3. A strange doorlatch

E. In the first paragraph the author seems to suggest that the descendants of the Dutch settlers were

_____ 1. a hard-working lot

_____ 2. believers in ghosts

_____ 3. gay and cheerful

F. In the second paragraph we get the impression that Ichabod Crane is

_____ 1. tall and gaunt

_____ 2. short and fat

_____ 3. not different from most people

G. In the third paragraph we learn that

_____ 1. corporal punishment was not permitted

_____ 2. Ichabod Crane was easygoing

_____ 3. the birch rod was used frequently

II. Other Features of the Writing

A. The author's point of view is

_____ 1. serious

_____ 2. factual

_____ 3. humorous

B. You sense early by the author's attitude that he

_____ 1. wants you to believe him

_____ 2. believes the story himself

_____ 3. just wants you to enjoy a fanciful tale

C. If we go beyond his words, we can conclude that the author is suggesting that

_____ 1. children should not be hit with birch rods

_____ 2. all Dutch people are highly superstitious

_____ 3. you should join him in having some fun

D. From the way he writes, we can judge that the author

_____ 1. can't take a joke

_____ 2. seems warm and friendly

_____ 3. talks like a stuffed shirt

ANSWERS: I.   A. 2,   B. 1,   C. 3,   D. 1,   E. 2,   F. 1,
G. 3.
II.   A. 3,   B. 3,   C. 3,   D. 2.

We will now examine the paragraphs one by one, with the aim of suggesting what you should have been looking for as you read. First, you want to prove to yourself that all good writing follows the pattern we have recommended. Secondly, since facts alone are not enough to enable you to meet the writer on equal terms, you want to be shown wherein the factors leading to appreciation and evaluation can be found. Finally, you will be getting your first demonstration of what it means to make a full-scale attack upon the contents of a selection.

First Paragraph

The job here is to tell something about the town where the story takes place. So you learn of its *drowsy* nature, the *marvelous beliefs* of its people, and one superstition in particular, the *Headless Horseman*. The topic, supporting, and concluding sentences have been used and have achieved their purpose. You don't concern yourself with a scientific analysis of the author's facts because he has already told you that you are going to read a story involving local superstitions. Therefore, you try to lose yourself in the fanciful tale about to unfold. You aren't ready yet to draw conclusions about Washington Irving's personality, but the mere suggestion of a rider without a head tells you that this writer has imagination, to say the least.

This is a lot to say about and see in a short paragraph, isn't it? Does it mean that when you read you must consciously look for topic, supporting, and concluding sentences? At first, yes. After you have practiced sufficiently, you will find these keys to understanding automatically. Should you be taking the other points mentioned into consideration simultaneously as you read? Again, yes. Are you thinking now that you are lucky enough when you get the main idea out of a paragraph, let alone additional things? That's reasonable, too. However, you have embarked upon this training program to *improve* your skills.

You wouldn't want to be short-changed. Through exercises supplied in this chapter and with additional practice on your own, you will gradually get into the habit of *looking for all the keys* to be found in a piece of writing. What it amounts to is your being able eventually to "size up" *what* is being said and *how* it is being said.

Second Paragraph

Once more the topic sentence introduces the subject that will be talked about—Ichabod Crane. There follow the supporting sentences, which give you an accurate picture of what he does for a living and what he looks like. By now also you have probably been amused by the references to *a mile out of his sleeves, served for shovels,* and *nose . . . like a weathercock.* You know, therefore, that you can expect further expressions of the author's sense of humor, and perhaps you have already begun to enjoy his easy, informal style. We have here an almost perfect blending of the structural elements that can be found in every skillfully written paragraph.

Third Paragraph

Again an almost perfect paragraph: the single important idea—a description of the schoolhouse and the activities of its occupants—the details, the flashes of humor, are all here. You can now, since your reading has ceased, step a bit farther back and ask yourself what Irving's overall purpose was in the first three paragraphs of his story. Obviously he wanted to introduce the main character and give us the setting of the story.

What if you had read the paragraphs without having alerted yourself to look for the keys to understanding and appreciation? Your rate might have suffered because you would have been unable to slide past words like *Hessian, wight, cognomen, eelpot,* without getting the uneasy feeling that you were missing something. As it is, you could concentrate on the total view of the selection and leave the vocabulary for some other time. Furthermore, you might have become confused by the long sentences, or you might have paid so much attention to the details that you would have missed the wit and charm of the story. But knowing what to look for makes it possible for you to plunge into a paragraph, take out of it what is necessary, and go on to the next without allowing yourself to be upset over small matters. You concern yourself with thoughts and ideas, not single words.

Knowing what you now do about writing techniques, you can begin to train yourself to keep in mind a set of guide questions that will help you find the keys to total comprehension of any material you read:

1. What is the author's **purpose?**
2. What is the **main idea** of each paragraph?
3. What **details** are significant?
4. What is the writer's **point of view?**
5. Can I **believe** him? Why?
6. Does he **suggest** anything beyond what he says?
7. Does his writing have some **special quality?**

Although we were able to get answers to all the guide questions in the selection from "Sleepy Hollow," it is not possible to do so with everything you read. You must first determine the *author's purpose.* Then you can decide what other questions are pertinent to that particular material. Let's see how this works with some typical selections.

Clever Young Man from Old Chatham

In old Chatham, so they say, there was a very clever young man. Among other things, he invented a new way to catch fish.

First, he dipped his hook into blackstrap molasses. (Or "long-tail sugar," as they used to say.) Then he cast his hook high into the air. This drew the bees. The bees stuck to the hook.

Next move, the clever young man heaved his bee-covered drail into the water. Up swam the fish, thinking the bees were big flies. But being in the water had made the bees very angry. They stung the fish to death.

Was not this young man from Chatham about as clever as they come?

———————

Fables and Foibles

A retired sea captain in a certain Cape Cod town was taking a walk along the beach one day. He was about to turn for the homeward stretch, when he saw two men a little farther ahead engaged in a rather heated discussion.

Quickening his pace, he neared them, and called out, "What's the trouble, men?"

"Well," said one of the men, "we were walking here together, when I saw this oyster that he has in his hand, and we both want it. I say it is mine because I saw it first."

"Not so!" hotly contended the other man. "He saw it first, that's true. But I was the one who ran and picked it up. So I say it is mine."

"Hmm!" said the old captain. "Would you like me to settle the argument?" To this proposal they agreed, and he said, "Let me have the oyster."

Taking the oyster, the captain pried it open, ate the oyster, and gave each contender half of the shell.

———

In the two tales above, the author's purpose is clear very early. When he says *so they say* in the first, and *in a certain Cape Cod town* in the other, you know at once that he is out to tell a fanciful or tall tale. This knowledge automatically eliminates from consideration all the other guide questions. No important ideas or details are going to be presented, and since the writer is spoofing, you need not concern yourself about his attitude or reliability. He has as much as warned you not to trust him. What he wants you to do is have a laugh. Certainly this kind of material can be read at your very fastest rate because there is little challenge to your comprehension. The same is true of all articles, stories, and books whose basic purpose is to amuse and entertain. You can rip right through them!

GUIDE QUESTIONS—EXERCISE 2

Here is an excerpt from a news article concerned with juvenile crime:

> Commissioner Jordan said he "deplored" the use of the problem as a potential issue by Republican opponents of Mayor Fenton.
>
> "This is a matter of life and public safety," he said. "It should not be exploited for political purposes."
>
> Although he deplored the injection of politics into the juvenile crime problem,

Mr. Fenton took occasion to point out that
the last Mayor to run with Republican
backing had reduced the size of the police
force.

Since this is a news article, you would know the purpose of the writer before you got to it because presumably
the job of a reporter is to present an objective summary
of the facts. Accordingly, you would certainly want to
absorb the main idea and important details of what he
said. However, you would miss something if you didn't
go beyond the facts.

The comment by the reporter, "Although he deplored
the injection of politics into the juvenile crime problem,"
indicates a considerable shortage of sympathy for the com-
missioner's statement. Whether the attitude is justified is
not the question. What is significant to you as a reader is
that your mind should be alert to a writer's point of view,
when he presents facts, so that you are not unconsciously
influenced in your own opinion. Therefore, the only question you would not use as a guide in material of this type
would be Number 7. Newspaper writing, except in features and editorials, usually follows a fairly regular pattern
and you need not look for individuality.

In fact, it is only when the reporter breaks the pattern
that you can get the answers to guide questions 4, 5, and
6. It is in the side remarks that slip out, so to speak, that
you can look for the point of view, reliability, and "anything beyond what he says." What party do you think this
paper might support?

Suppose, as another example, you were reading a summary of a day's legislative activities and the statements of
a particular speaker were called "arrogant," or he was
described as "chubby and rumpled." Certainly the terms
referring to manner of speech and personal appearance
do not conceal the reporter's point of view. To someone

on the other side of the fence, the same speaker might have seemed "determined" and "delightfully informal."

You can therefore read news articles rather quickly, too, since the main ideas are suggested by the headlines, strongly stated in the opening sentence or two, and merely repeated in detail in the paragraphs that follow. But be on the lookout for the little asides that give away the attitude of the writer.

GUIDE QUESTIONS—EXERCISE 3

Misguided Missiles

The modern automobile is a triumph of engineering, quick to respond to the will of the driver. Unfortunately, the design of the driver has not kept pace.

The Travelers Insurance Company reports that 35,500 people died in traffic accidents in 1954 with almost two million injured. Excessive speed contributed to about 50% of the accidents, with recklessness and driving on the wrong side of the road closely following.

It's not the new driver who causes most harm; 97% of drivers in accidents have been driving over a year. Drivers under 25 were involved in more than their proportionate share of accidents. And for the age-old controversy: male drivers accounted for 91% of fatal accidents.

Cars were in good mechanical condition as a whole. If the care of the driver matched the care of his car, we would have 91% fewer accidents.

It is sad that for 13,980 drivers Saturday and Sunday became days of permanent rest. The middle of the week is much safer. By far most accidents per cars on the road occurred in the dark, between 1:00 A.M. and 6:00 A.M. Dry roads, fair weather and careless driving seem to go together.

104

Auto deaths have decreased slightly. But there are now roughly double the cars on the road, and deaths per 100,-000 vehicles declined about 50%.

Statistics reveal that the decrease came about, not because of our drivers, but in spite of them. The report shows that the ratios of causes of accidents do not substantially differ from figures of previous years. The conclusion is unmistakable that the decrease in deaths is due far more to mechanical and medical progress than to a fundamental change in driver attitude.

*   *   *

Since the purpose of the writer, as revealed in the very first paragraph, is to express an opinion about the causes of accidents, you immediately set yourself to use all the guide questions, except possibly the last. If there is something distinctive about the style it will be incidental, since the subject does not lend itself readily to creative expression. You want to get the main ideas, of course, but your attention to the details should be limited to getting an impression rather than attempting the almost impossible task of memorizing the figures. You want to check the reliability of the writer so that you can determine whether the conclusions are justified. Here's how that is done.

If the author were an acknowledged authority in the subject area, you might be inclined to accept at face value much of what is said. However, since this is not a signed article, you must look to other sources. What other evidence is there to support the writer's position? The statistics quoted from a reliable company indicate that there was research on the topic and ordinarily should influence you favorably regarding point of view and reliability.

Even under the latter circumstances, you must be careful. "The Devil can cite the Scriptures to suit his own ends." I neither want to call the writer a devil nor get into a controversy over male and female drivers, but let's examine one of the statistics from the point of view of whether numbers always tell the whole truth. You read that male drivers account for 91 per cent of fatal accidents. Has the writer told you what percentage of *all* drivers are male? Has he indicated whether some of the male drivers got into accidents because they were trying to avoid female drivers (Heaven help me)? Has he taken into consideration the hazardous occupations of men that might account for their greater incidence of fatalities— auto-racing, bus and truck driving, venturing forth on icy roads, ambulance and other emergency-vehicle driving that requires speed to get to a destination?

Later on in the article, is the author's conclusion that the decrease in deaths is due to mechanical and medical progress an acceptable one? Surely modern cars on new parkways go faster than ever, and doctors can use their new techniques to heal the victims but cannot prevent the accidents. Again, let me repeat, I am not quarreling with the writer or the ladies (could the author have been one?), but I am pointing out to you that you must look for statistics and proof, and you do not accept what you read unless all sides of the problem have been covered. In material of this kind, your guide questions are very valuable. They force you to *think with the writer* and prevent you from accepting the main ideas and details without argument.

GUIDE QUESTIONS—EXERCISE 4

So far we have been concentrating on articles that stress the importance of going beyond the facts or ignoring them altogether. We haven't done much with the last guide question, which refers to the author's style or personality. In the following passage you will have the opportunity to see how the latter is of particular importance.

The summer is moving along. It is going by at a rate calling to mind the speed of light. The Fourth of July is over now, as well as two pleasant trips to Jones Beach and half a dozen tasty picnics. The picturesque road which was found last year has been traveled again, although over the winter it has become a superhighway feeder. However, there must be other picturesque roads, and perhaps one of them will be discovered before the summer is over. The discovery had best be soon, though, for the days of the summer are numbered. They are flying by, and the comparison which at once comes to mind is the speed of light. They are vanishing as though it were nobody's business, whereas the reverse of that clearly is the truth. They must be stopped somehow. As they say in the automotive trades, their speed of passage must be decelerated. For, to be honest, unless the flying summer is slowed abruptly, this summer's planned project will not be completed. At the moment, it is not nearly as finished as is the summer. This is deplorable, and eventually will be causing loose talk.

That project was a product of the winter. Back in February there was a particularly nasty day. The wind blew, there was snow, the furnace failed to function and the radiator of the car cracked from freezing. Late in the afternoon the mind had enough of contemplating such a day, and so it looked forward to the summer. Since the mind is an active one, it did not just scheme to lie about in the sun, dozing the hours away. Instead of this lazy approach, it made plans for improvements about the place. It considered painting the outside of the house; it considered painting the trim alone. It considered widening the vegetable garden and lengthening the flower garden, and building a stone wall along the back of the property and building an outdoor fireplace near the wall. At the end of that February day all of these things were jotted down in the Diary under the heading Summer Projects. Unfortunately, the Projects also were announced publicly, at dinner. That was bad.

Spring came, and then came the summer. What with one thing and another, it was deemed best not to use the scattershot system of dealing with the Summer Projects. One by one, those deemed of lesser importance were dropped. Painting the house was the first to be abandoned, and after that, painting the trim. Although there was some rude talk about it at the evening dinner table, it should have been obvious that the trim and the house belonged together, and should be painted together, some other summer. Widening the vegetable garden then was abandoned, and not altogether because the Yankees were having a spirited double-header on the afternoon work was supposed to begin. Lengthening the flower garden happened to coincide with a dandy single game, which was a raw coincidence, leaving the garden the size it was before. Building the stone wall looked—well, the specifications for the Great Wall of China may have called for more stone, but probably not. That left, as Project—in the singular—the fireplace.

Now the summer is flying by. It is moving along at a rate akin to the speed of light. The Fourth of July has gone, as well as a couple of Jones Beach excursions and some tasty picnics. About these picnics, it must be said at once that cold foods were involved, not grilled ones. The fireplace still is in the construction stage; indeed there are those of small courtesy who say that it merely is in the planning stage. Obviously this is unfair, for are the stones not piled ready in a little mound, and are not the ingredients of concrete stored in the garage? All that is lacking to make the fireplace a finished Project is another summer. One perhaps slightly longer than this one. And one which doesn't travel so rapidly through space.

*　　　*　　　*

This author was interested mainly in having a pleasant chat with his reader. You can almost picture him dressed in a pair of old trousers and an open-collared shirt; sitting comfortably, drink in hand, on his outdoor patio; and amiably talking about those domestic shortcomings that are common to all of us. To enjoy this kind of article, you must set your mind to comparing your own experiences with those of the writer. You want to see whether his words express colorfully the very things you have often thought of. You aren't interested in his main ideas, details, reliability, or hidden meanings so much as you are in the personality that comes through in his style of writing.

You observe his technique of ending a paragraph with a very short sentence that nonetheless conveys a world of meaning: "This is deplorable, and eventually will be causing loose talk," "That was bad," and "That left, as Project —in the singular—the fireplace." You visualize the pictures he continually creates: "Half a dozen tasty picnics," "The wind blew, there was snow, the furnace failed to function," "lie about in the sun, dozing the hours away," and "specifications for the Great Wall of China may have called for more stone." His references to a "spirited double-header" and a "dandy single game" give you an inkling of his many-sided interests. He deliberately repeats so that you can be sure that this is not the first time the summer projects have fallen by the wayside.

Style is the trade-mark of good writers. If a writer has developed a distinctive style, it is as revealing of his personality as is his manner of talking, eating, dressing, or dancing. You decide that an individual is rather formal because you never hear him use slang or colloquialisms and his attitude toward even trivial things is too intense. Another will strike you as being informal and friendly because of his willingness to use any expression so long as it is the best for a particular thought and because he regards all matters within their proper proportions. Much of your delight from reading can come in meeting interesting people through their articles and stories. And of course, your appreciation of their material is so much the greater when you know what to look for. Isn't this concept equally true when you look at a painting, listen to some fine music, or watch a baseball game?

The selections we have just reviewed were designed to show you how to set your mind to thinking about values in your reading that go beyond just the main ideas and details. I readily grant that we have just about scratched the surface of developing judgment of a writer's attitude, motives, and style, as well as his content. However, you can use this as a start. As you read more, you will see more, and your reactions will become sharper and deeper.

Will this search for full comprehension slow you up? On the contrary! When you know in advance what you should get out of an article, story, or book, you are in a position to dictate your own speed. This is the best way to learn when to vary your reading rate. The author's purpose and the pertinent guide questions will enable you to judge intelligently the proper amount of time to spend upon a given selection. You will get into the material and stay there just long enough to get out of it what is of value. If, for instance, you start a novel that you have wanted to read, but find that the author is spending a lot of time establishing his background for the story, you may be tempted to set the book aside because you haven't the desire to wade through the dull introductory chapters. With your ability to recognize the purpose of a writer and thus gauge how and where to center your attention, you can knife through the dead spots and even skip a page or two without losing much.

Make it a practice to reread, from time to time, our analyses of the "Sleepy Hollow" excerpt and the selections just concluded. You will be helping your mind gradually acquire what the psychologists call the proper "mental set." It will LOOK FOR THE KEYS, and find them!

We are now ready for the exercises that will help you use full comprehension. The selections will be graded in difficulty, getting harder as you proceed. Don't try to push your rate just yet. You may even find it slowing up a bit. Don't worry about that. As you become more expert in picking out the essential ideas and characteristics of the practice paragraphs, your speed will automatically increase. In the long run, as we've said, because of your improved comprehension, it will be easier than ever to push yourself.

We will start modestly. Our first few exercises will require that you find only the main ideas and important details. Once you have developed the technique of LOOKING FOR THE KEYS through the topic, supporting, and concluding sentences in the paragraphs, you will be able to go on to the kind of *full-comprehension* test you took in connection with "The Legend of Sleepy Hollow." As usual, do not attempt to do all the exercises in one session. Wait for the complete instructions about your Daily Plan in Chapter X.

COMPREHENSION EXERCISE 1

Read each paragraph carefully, LOOK FOR THE KEYS, and then answer the questions that follow.

a. Almost without exception boat owners are rabid camera fans. Unfortunately, however, many of the boating enthusiasts who like to click an occasional shutter find that the results they achieve leave something to be desired. They forget that the camera's eye works on principles similar to their own, and that a bright sunlit day on the water that causes them to squint and reach for colored glasses also has an adverse effect on the film in the camera unless certain precautions are taken. Light on the water acquires an almost unbelievable intensity. A technic that would produce satisfactory results ashore is entirely unsuited to boating pictures.

The title below that best expresses the ideas of this paragraph is

_____ 1. Water colors
_____ 2. Photography on the water
_____ 3. Intensity of light on the water
_____ 4. How the camera's eye works
_____ 5. Camera technic

The writer emphasizes that pictures taken on boats are often spoiled by the

_____ 1. overenthusiasm of the photographer
_____ 2. motion of the boat
_____ 3. lack of a color filter
_____ 4. too bright light
_____ 5. use of the wrong film

b. In no field of history has the search for logical explanation been so diligent as in the study of the decline and fall of the Roman Empire. The only known instance of the decay of a more or less universal civilization, it might serve as something of an object lesson to our own; accordingly it has been very thoroughly studied, and the attempt to explain it has engaged some of the ablest historians who ever wrote. Almost any orator or politician can tell you why Rome fell, but the men who know most about it are not so ready with glib explanations. Even they must admit at critical moments the decisive interposition of Chance.

The title that best expresses the ideas of this paragraph is

_____ 1. The Roman Empire

_____ 2. Studying reasons for the decline and fall of the Roman Empire

_____ 3. Causes for the decline

_____ 4. Chance is decisive

_____ 5. Able historians know why Rome fell

The fall of the Roman Empire has been thoroughly studied because

_____ 1. it may serve as a lesson to us

_____ 2. it affected the lives of so many people

_____ 3. it was so unusual

_____ 4. Rome was the greatest empire the world has known

_____ 5. detailed records are readily available

People who know most about the fall of the Roman Empire

_____ 1. think politicians were its chief cause

_____ 2. are uncertain as to its cause

_____ 3. prepare object lessons from it

_____ 4. give ready explanations of it

_____ 5. have been able to learn little about it

c. The artist of the Renaissance was an all-round man. From his studio one could order a painting for the church altar, a carved wedding chest, a silver ewer, or a crucifix. The master of the workshop might be sculpturing a Venus for the Duke's garden while his apprentices were roughing-out a reredos for the new chapel. Many of the well-known painters of that golden period were goldsmiths, armorers, workers in glass, enamel or iron. The engineer was artist and the artist was engineer. The great Leonardo, famous today as the painter of "The Last Supper" and "Mona Lisa," was perhaps equally well known in the sixteenth century for his engineering projects and his scientific experiments. Our own Thomas A. Edison pronounced him the greatest inventive genius of his time.

The title below that best expresses the ideas of this paragraph is

_____ 1. The great Leonardo

_____ 2. Edison and sixteenth-century scientists

_____ 3. The golden period

_____ 4. Masters and apprentices

_____ 5. Renaissance artists

Leonardo was famed as

_____ 1. a scientist

_____ 2. an electrician

_____ 3. a worker in glass

_____ 4. a railroad engineer

_____ 5. an apprentice

d. Just why some individuals choose one way of adjusting to their difficulties and others choose other ways is not known. Yet what an individual does when he is thwarted remains a reasonably good key to the understanding of his personality. If his responses to thwartings are emotional explosions and irrational excuses, he is tending to live in an unreal world. He may need help to regain the world of reality, the cause-and-effect world recognized by generations of thinkers and scientists. Perhaps he needs encouragement to redouble his efforts. Perhaps, on the other hand, he is striving for the impossible and needs to substitute a worthwhile activity within the range of his abilities. It is the part of wisdom to learn the nature of the world and of oneself in relation to it and to meet each situation as intelligently and as adequately as one can.

The title that best expresses the ideas of this paragraph is

_____ 1. Adjusting to life

_____ 2. Escape from reality

_____ 3. The importance of personality

_____ 4. Emotional control

_____ 5. The real nature of the world

The writer argues that all should

_____ 1. substitute new activities for old

_____ 2. redouble their efforts

_____ 3. analyze their relation to the world

_____ 4. seek encouragement from others
_____ 5. avoid thwartings

ANSWERS: a. 2, 4; b. 2, 1, 2; c. 5, 1; d. 1, 3.

COMPREHENSION EXERCISE 2

This exercise will test your ability to see the close relationship that must exist between the details of a paragraph and the topic sentence. It will train you to detect where a writer has gone off his subject. Such knowledge is important as it prevents you from becoming confused by poor paragraph construction and offers you a certain indication that an author is inept and is probably not worth reading!

After the topic sentence, you will find the remaining sentences *numbered*. Circle the numbers of those sentences that do not belong because they seem to have no contributing connection to the main idea of the paragraph.

Three English officers and a group of natives were hunting for two lions that had made a raid upon a village the night before. (1) In the course of the day, one of the savage pair was killed, but the other escaped to the jungle. (2) Fanning out, the hunters proceeded cautiously. (3) After a few steps, one of them, the lieutenant, caught a glimpse of the lion and instantly fired, thus enraging the beast so that it rushed toward him at full speed. (4) The officer was wearing a regular khaki military outfit. (5) Captain Woodhouse saw the movement and knew that if he tried to get into a better position for firing, he would put himself directly in the way of the charge. (6) He decided to stand still, trusting the lion would pass close by, unaware of him, and that he could then perhaps shoot to advantage. (7) But he was deceived. (8) The furious animal saw him, and flew at him with a dreadful roar. (9) The lion is considered to be the king of the beasts of Africa. (10) In an instant, the rifle was broken and thrown out of the captain's hand, his left arm at the same moment being seized by the claws and his right by the teeth of his antagonist. (11) Rifles can be broken by one swipe of a lion's paw.

ANSWERS: You should have circled these numbers: 4, 9, 11. Did you notice how the proper concluding sentence of this paragraph provides a perfect lead into the next one? So that you do not remain in frustrated suspense, let me assure you that the captain, somewhat the worse for wear, was rescued by other members of the party.

COMPREHENSION EXERCISE 3

In the following article, the paragraphs have been numbered. After you have finished your reading, number the subtitles below the selection to match the numbers of the paragraphs. For example, if you think the first subtitle fits the first paragraph, write 1 in the space provided. This gives you further training in selecting main ideas. Since your purpose here is to get to the main idea, you will want to read rather quickly so that the details do not interfere. The title has deliberately been omitted, and you will be asked to supply one later.

*   *   *

[1.] Many people believe the glare from snow causes snowblindness. Yet, dark glasses or not, they find themselves suffering from headaches and watering eyes, and even snowblindness, when exposed to several hours of "snow" light.

[2.] The United States Army has now determined that glare from snow does not cause snowblindness in troops operating in a snow-covered country. Rather, a man's eyes frequently find nothing to focus on in a broad expanse of barren snow-covered terrain. So his gaze continually shifts and jumps back and forth over the entire landscape in search of something to look at. Finding nothing, hour after hour, the eyes never stop searching and the eyeballs become sore and the eye muscles ache. Nature offsets this irritation by producing more and more fluid which covers the eyeball. The fluid covers the eyeball in increasing quantity until vision blurs, then is obscured, and the result is total, even though temporary, snowblindness.

[3.] Experiments led the Army to a simple method of overcoming this problem. Scouts ahead of a main body of troops are trained to shake snow from evergreen bushes, creating a dotted line as they cross completely snow-covered landscape. Even the scouts throw lightweight, dark-colored objects ahead on which they too can focus. The men following can then see something. Their gaze is arrested. Their eyes focus on a bush and, having found something to see, stop scouring the snow-blanketed landscape. By focusing their attention on one object, one at a time, the men can cross the snow without becoming hopelessly snowblind or lost. The problem of crossing a solid white terrain is helped.

Now number the subtitles so that they match the numbers of the paragraphs.

_____ Causes of snowblindness
_____ Traveling the Arctic waste

_____ A common wrong idea

_____ The need for dark glasses

_____ The solution to snowblindness

A good title for the entire selection would be

_____ 1. The United States Army

_____ 2. Winter problems

_____ 3. People's misconceptions

_____ 4. Causes and cures of snowblindness

_____ 5. The duties of scouts

ANSWERS: __2__ Causes of snowblindness

__1__ A common wrong idea

__3__ The solution to snowblindness

The best title is 4.

COMPREHENSION EXERCISE 4

This exercise and the ones that follow bring you to the training for full comprehension. They will give you practice in recognizing all the features suggested by our guide questions that should be observed by the reader in addition to main ideas and details. As you read the selection, keep in mind the need for ascertaining not only *what* the writer says but *how* he says it.

Kids, Goats, and Bees

There's a family in Falmouth whose lively types of animal and insect life keep things hopping. The master of the situation (?) got some goats last year to spare him from having to mow his lawn, or so his family declares. Now, he confesses, he still has to mow the lawn; in addition he has to milk the goats.

He also asserts a fondness for goats' milk, and his mother and sister agree enthusiastically with him on this point, but remark, "We simply prefer our tea and coffee black."

He insists that his goats are gentle creatures, but his wife was the butt of a misunderstanding about this last summer, when one of the goats proved the point—without doing any serious harm.

When this summer five puppies entered the scene, they equaled the number of cats in the family. Since then, a hive of bees has joined the ranks. One of the cats, Rusty, tried to strike up a speaking acquaintance with the hive, and from the fact that she is still running in an opposite direction, has proved that there is no rust in her joints.

The family insist, without kidding, that the goats are the most intelligent of all their livestock, and have never eaten shirts off the clothesline, but admit that one did once sample the coat an innocent bystander was wearing.

I. Main ideas and details

A. Another good title for this selection would be

_____ 1. Goat's milk
_____ 2. A family that likes pets
_____ 3. A home-grown lawn mower
_____ 4. A silly group of people
_____ 5. Pets offer many problems

B. The wife

_____ 1. likes goats
_____ 2. was once butted by a goat
_____ 3. prefers her coffee black

_____ 4. was stung by a bee

_____ 5. wants to get rid of the pets

C. The family's attitude toward the pets is

_____ 1. indifferent

_____ 2. hostile

_____ 3. favorable

_____ 4. worried

_____ 5. puzzled

II. *Other features*

A. The writer's primary purpose is to

_____ 1. inform

_____ 2. ridicule

_____ 3. amuse

_____ 4. condemn

_____ 5. praise

B. The writer's point of view is that of

_____ 1. scientific accuracy

_____ 2. serious analysis

_____ 3. crusading zeal

_____ 4. amiable good humor

_____ 5. violent antagonism

C. The writer achieves a light touch in his style by

_____ 1. cracking jokes

_____ 2. poking cruel fun

_____ 3. pretending to be matter-of-fact

_____ 4. stressing human weakness

_____ 5. using ordinary language

D. The two guide questions that are least important in analyzing this piece are

_____ 1. purpose
_____ 2. main ideas
_____ 3. details
_____ 4. point of view
_____ 5. reliability
_____ 6. hidden meanings
_____ 7. style

ANSWERS: I.   A. 2,   B. 2,   C. 3.
          II.   A. 3,   B. 4,   C. 3,   D. 5, 6.

Notes on the answers

II. C. The technique employed by the writer is similar to that of the straight-faced comedians of stage and screen. They don't "pull" a laugh, but they arrange their remarks so that the humor comes out of an almost serious description of an absurd situation. They also do not scorn the lowly pun—a play on words like "his wife was the *butt* of a misunderstanding."

II. D. In an article written for pure entertainment, the reader should not be concerned with looking deeply into the meaning, nor should he wonder whether the writer is telling the truth.

COMPREHENSION EXERCISE 5

Here again you ascertain the writer's purpose as soon as you can and then LOOK FOR THE KEYS that you consider important in this selection.

You have only two chances in a million to find a pearl in the 10 million bushels of oysters eaten each year in this country.

This large quantity of oysters, you may not know, is not the result of just fishing, but farming. Early in the spring an oyster farmer prepares his beds, then cultivates and harvests his crops. After buying or renting bay bottoms from cities, which by law own one to three miles out, the oysterman prepares the ground. He clears the bottom of all debris and spreads it with old opened oyster shells. This "clutch," which is spread where natural or planted beds of adult oysters are located, provides a hard surface for baby oysters to cling to. May to September is the spawning season and oysters are not as palatable then, though just as good. That is one reason fewer are eaten in the months without "R." The other reason is it gives a chance to conserve the industry for future seasons.

Baby oysters come from fertilized eggs dropped at the rate of 50 million a year by the female oyster. So small are the eggs that a quart could hold all the eggs needed to supply the nation's annual crop.

The eggs grow bivalved shells in 24 hours and begin swimming. Soon they cement themselves to the shells. By the time the new oysters grow to the size of your thumbnail, in about six months, they're crowding each other. Then the oyster farmer has to separate and replant them or their growth is retarded. So he transplants them to growing grounds, often miles away. Growing ground is chosen for availability of food particles and its immunity from storm damage, often 15 to 50 feet below the surface. A combination of fresh and salt water is best.

In the growing beds oysters are left undisturbed except

for periodic inspection to look out for starfish and snails, oysters' mortal enemies.

In their third year oysters are large enough to harvest. Boats head out for the beds marked with long poles sticking out above the water. Huge dredges with steel teeth, lowered over the sides, drag along the bottom gathering up the oysters into nets.

Oyster beds are found along the Atlantic, Gulf and Pacific shores. The largest crop comes from Chesapeake Bay; the best growing ground is now considered to be the Connecticut shore.

I. Main ideas and details

   A. Another title for the selection could be

   _____ 1. Growing cultivated oysters

   _____ 2. An oyster's mortal enemy

   _____ 3. Dredging for oysters

   _____ 4. Where the best oyster beds are

   _____ 5. Baby oysters

   B. The main idea of the second paragraph is

   _____ 1. spreading "clutches"

   _____ 2. months without an "R"

   _____ 3. bay bottoms

   _____ 4. oyster farming

   _____ 5. adult and baby oysters

   C. We are told that oysters

   _____ 1. grow very rapidly in size

   _____ 2. grow best on the surface

_____ 3. drop single eggs

_____ 4. require several years to grow large

_____ 5. are harvested by hand

D. *A clutch is*

_____ 1. part of an automobile

_____ 2. a bed of old oyster shells

_____ 3. a transplanting

_____ 4. a hard grip

_____ 5. a kind of dredge

II. *Other features*

A. The author's purpose was to

_____ 1. prove he likes oysters

_____ 2. criticize oyster farming

_____ 3. entertain the reader

_____ 4. prove he is a scientist

_____ 5. describe oysters' habits

B. The author's style shows an effort to be

_____ 1. personal

_____ 2. formal

_____ 3. superior

_____ 4. cold

_____ 5. vulgar

C. The details in the selection should be

_____ 1. ignored completely

_____ 2. memorized

_____ 3. checked with references

_____ 4. read quickly

_____ 5. studied very carefully

D. The three guide questions that are least important here are

_____ 1. purpose

_____ 2. main ideas

_____ 3. details

_____ 4. point of view

_____ 5. reliability

_____ 6. hidden meanings

_____ 7. style

ANSWERS: I. A. 1, B. 4, C. 4, D. 2.

            II. A. 3, B. 1, C. 4, D. 4, 5, 6.

Notes on the answers

II. A. The writer is not attempting to present a textbook study but is offering the material purely for appreciation and interest.

II. B. The use of "you may not know" and "size of your thumbnail" indicates the desire of the writer to make the style personal.

II. C. Since you are reading this kind of article solely for entertainment, you observe the details but do not linger over them.

II. D. There can be no hidden meanings in such a discussion of oysters, and it can be safely assumed that the writer checked his facts.

Up to this point we have been considering the *writer's* purpose, asking you to ascertain it early and then decide how you are going to read his material and which of the guide questions you will need to apply. However, it is important to point out that there will be occasions when *your* purpose will differ from the writer's. For instance, let us suppose that some evening, having nothing else to read, you select a volume of an encyclopedia and glance through it casually, picking up bits here and there. Now, the writers of such articles undoubtedly had in mind that their material was to be used primarily in scholarly research. In this case, your purpose and the writer's would be completely different. Similarly, you might read an article like the one on oysters with the express purpose of preparing for some examination. The details then would be of great importance to you.

What you do, of course, when there is this difference between your purpose and the author's, is to let yours be the determining factor in so far as speed and the guide questions are concerned. However, you should not make the mistake of going to the wrong material to suit your need. In general, when you are reading for information or serious study, you should select articles and books that have been written carefully and authoritatively. And when you are reading for relaxation and enjoyment, you will want to turn to lighter materials. For the average reader, a good guide to whether he has selected appropriate reading matter is the closeness with which his purpose and the writer's agree.

COMPREHENSION EXERCISES 6 AND 7

The next two selections should prove to be quite interesting for you. The first is a poem written by a sixteen-year-old boy, who won a national contest with his effort, and the second is a letter written by his twenty-one-year-old brother after the latter had read the poetry while he was on Army duty in Europe. Not only will these pieces be a change from the literary forms we have been using, but they will give you the opportunity to make certain comparisons between the writers. You will probably want to read the poem somewhat more slowly than the letter.

Death

BY STEPHEN M. SELTZER

Praise Death!
Death is not to be feared,
Death is the end of fear.
Life—fearful and unpredictable flows into Death.
Death, absolute Death!

As the short lived spray of the ocean melts finally
    into the sea,
People once more become part of the whole
In Death.
In the long, dreamless sleep, the many "I's" fall into
    nothingness.
Death, the equalizer!
Neither reward nor revenge in Death—
Just peaceful non-existence.
Death, triumphant Death!

The Letter

BY HOWARD N. SELTZER

Hi Steve,

Well, you seem to have grown quite perceptive in your usual quiet way. I'm referring to your poem, of course. It's good, if the praise of a sparsely educated layman means anything. My experience in the field of poesy is rather limited; almost non-existent except for what Mother Casey forced through my iron-bound head.

You seem to be quite knowledgeable on the subject, and while I don't understand how you got that way, I envy your philosophy.

I can't accept death as an "equalizer," a time of peace eternal or an ending of mortal care and terror. For me it is a thing to be feared, avoided, cheated at any price. It is a final and eternal ending, a finish to laughter and a farewell to sound and color and texture, and all the small pleasures that make life worth the living.

It's a selfish attitude at best, but it's mine, and I'm stuck with it. The simple pleasures that are nothing more than the candy-coating on the pill, the spice on the cake, emotional deodorants, so to speak, are well worth the grub-like, terrible routine that most of us live our lives in.

As a case in point, I'm going to an extreme but it's a good example. After a long, queasy flight in a plane, when the order comes to "stand"—that's a partial death, a relaxation of senses, a numbing to what is ahead. One is very calm, looking around with the detached air of a slightly-intoxicated idiot, but conscious only of the man ahead and the door. It's a sort of self-induced hypnosis, an extreme concentration wherein all action, though newly-learned, is instinctive. As you leave the door, the fear comes back and the question—will it happen this time? Then you know. In four seconds you know. Subjectively though it is longer. It can be your lifetime. You're on the ground now. Completely and utterly relaxed. You roll your 'chute and carry it to the truck, meeting friends on the way, a man among men. You sit down and maybe light a cigarette, listening to the "jump" stories, funny and not so funny. The sun is on your back and the little flying things are playing in a field in front of you. The consciousness, the sensuality, the extreme pleasure of simple movement are seldom so sharply defined as now. Any simple little thing, such as gazing at your dirty fingernails, is luxury.

You have avoided the finality once more. Perhaps you won't next time, but this feeling, this primitive vice is well worth it.

This is the old Cornball signing off. Take it cool.

Howard

I. Main ideas and details

  A. The poet sees death as

    _____ 1. democratic in some ways
    _____ 2. an enemy
    _____ 3. something to be feared
    _____ 4. welcome
    _____ 5. tragic

  B. The letter writer regards death with

    _____ 1. indifference
    _____ 2. fear
    _____ 3. anticipation
    _____ 4. cowardice
    _____ 5. contempt

  C. The letter writer is

    _____ 1. an aviator
    _____ 2. a bombardier
    _____ 3. a paratrooper

_____ 4. a diver

_____ 5. a navigator

D. The letter writer

_____ 1. agrees with his brother

_____ 2. differs sharply

_____ 3. doesn't care one way or the other

_____ 4. considers him silly

_____ 5. agrees only in part

II. Other features

A. The poet's purpose is to

_____ 1. amuse

_____ 2. depress

_____ 3. uplift the hopeless

_____ 4. express his feelings

_____ 5. encourage suicide

B. The letter writer's purpose is to

_____ 1. explain his reactions to the subject

_____ 2. teach his brother a lesson

_____ 3. show how wrong his brother is

_____ 4. glorify his own occupation

_____ 5. scold his brother

C. If we read deeply into the poem we find feelings of

_____ 1. puzzlement

_____ 2. insecurity

_____ 3. insincerity

_____ 4. pride

_____ 5. superiority

D. If we read deeply into the letter we find that the author

    _____ 1. likes his fingernails
    _____ 2. is afraid of life
    _____ 3. wants to be a hero
    _____ 4. enjoys his work
    _____ 5. wishes he were home

E. The poet's style is

    _____ 1. gay
    _____ 2. youthful
    _____ 3. shallow
    _____ 4. serious
    _____ 5. ordinary

F. The letter writer's style is

    _____ 1. dull
    _____ 2. imaginative
    _____ 3. flowery
    _____ 4. unclear
    _____ 5. immature

G. The guide question that obviously need not be asked about either piece is

    _____ 1. purpose
    _____ 2. main ideas
    _____ 3. details
    _____ 4. point of view
    _____ 5. reliability
    _____ 6. hidden meanings
    _____ 7. style

ANSWERS: I.   A. 1,   B. 2,   C. 3,   D. 2.
              II. A. 4,   B. 1,   C. 2,   D. 5,   E. 4,   F. 2,
                   G. 5.

Notes on the answers

II. A. The poet is not trying to influence the reader, but just tell how a young boy feels when he begins to give serious thought to a subject that troubles us all.

II. C. A sixteen-year-old boy who has not yet achieved station in life may be concerned about the "I's," and their relationship to his own identity. Will he amount to something? Will he be successful? There is almost a sense of security in the facelessness of death. This is a normal problem of adolescence.

II. F. The highly imaginative quality of the letter comes through in the writer's attention to detail about nature, his emotions, the small things about his existence.

II. G. Certainly since each is writing about his innermost feelings, we can assume sincerity and truth.

Which of the brothers is the better writer? I'm not going to answer this for you, but you might find it stimulating to discuss your choice with another person. You would, of course, have to point to specific qualities of the writing technique of either to support your position. This sort of discussion would give you valuable training. The more you study the tools of writing the better you are able to recognize a good piece of work and the deeper becomes your appreciation of the things you read.

COMPREHENSION EXERCISE 8

Here is an editorial from a Southern newspaper. It is a splendid example of how attention only to ideas and details would make it difficult for the reader to enjoy the piece for its other features, which are far more important.

133

Peck of Trouble Looms in Abandoning Bushel

There's mischief afoot. They're tampering with the measuring system, trying to replace the bushel with the hundredweight.

It's all a part of a foreign plot to eventually substitute the metric system, common in Europe and over the rest of the world, for our American standard of weights and measures. It is all being attempted in the name of simplicity, but what is more complicated than the meter, the basic unit of measurement under the system? The meter is defined as approximately "one ten-millionth part of the distance measured on a meridian from the equator to the pole. . . ." Anybody got a slide rule?

The hundredweight, they tell us, is being chosen to give us uniformity of measurement, because the weight of a bushel varies from state to state. That's well and good, but who says everybody agrees on the weight of a hundredweight? In England a hundredweight comes to 112 avoirdupois pounds, while in this country it tips the scale at 100 pounds. Now what's to keep this difference of opinion of the size of a hundredweight from cropping up in this country?

That's not all the difficulty involved, either. There's the loss to the language. Suppose hundredweight replaces bushel. Can you imagine anyone saying, "I love you a hundredweight and a peck," or a youngster deriding a "butter-fingered" ball player with, "Why you couldn't catch a ball with a hundredweight basket." And what about the Biblical passage? Shall it become, "Neither do men light a candle and put it under a hundredweight"?

Be it known anybody who tries to remove the bushel

from the channels of commerce, and consequently from our language, is in for a peck of trouble.

———

I. Main ideas and details

A. The main point of the writer is that

_____ 1. foreigners are mischievous

_____ 2. the new system of measurement will be good

_____ 3. the old system has serious defects

_____ 4. the change will result in no improvement

_____ 5. there is no agreement on how heavy a hundredweight is

B. The reason the change is advocated in this country is that there is

_____ 1. improper understanding of a bushel

_____ 2. lack of uniformity in bushel weights

_____ 3. better sense to the hundredweight

_____ 4. the need for a change

_____ 5. legislation pending

C. The change, according to the writer, will also introduce problems of

_____ 1. language

_____ 2. interstate commerce

_____ 3. international law

_____ 4. import duties

_____ 5. rural finance

II. Other features

A. The writer's purpose is to

_____ 1. offer savage criticism

_____ 2. support the movement for change

_____ 3. disapprove the change on patriotic grounds

_____ 4. furnish half-serious, half-comic opposition

_____ 5. show he doesn't care

B. The writer apparently is different from these people who favor products and ideas just because they are

_____ 1. local

_____ 2. scientific

_____ 3. imported

_____ 4. new

_____ 5. old

C. The writer's point of view shows his ability not to make

_____ 1. enemies

_____ 2. friends

_____ 3. trouble

_____ 4. mountains out of molehills

_____ 5. fun

D. The writer's use of the pun (play on words) in the title and text of the article gives his style

_____ 1. an ungrammatical construction

_____ 2. a humorous quality

_____ 3. a loose quality

136

_____ 4. a lack of clarity

_____ 5. a solemn touch

E. The guide question that is least important in analyzing this selection is

_____ 1. purpose

_____ 2. main ideas

_____ 3. details

_____ 4. point of view

_____ 5. reliability

_____ 6. hidden meanings

_____ 7. style

ANSWERS: I. A. 4, B. 2, C. 1.
          II. A. 4, B. 3, C. 4, D. 2, E. 5.

Notes on the answers

II. A. Although the article is obviously written in a humorous vein, the author is definitely opposed to the idea of a measurement change. His technique of objecting is used frequently by skilled writers. They reduce a suggestion to laughter and thus destroy its serious influence on the reader.

II. B. The answer here requires a little digging. One can detect a strong rejection of the idea that things abroad are done better.

II. E. You don't worry about the writer's reliability since he presents easily checked facts and his purpose is not scientific accuracy.

*   *   *

You will recall that at the beginning of this chapter you were told that improved comprehension can have a favorable effect on your reading rate. It should be clear to you now that the use of the guide questions to help you FIND THE KEYS contributes greatly to your deciding how fast you should read a particular selection. Thus by training yourself to allow what you are looking for to determine how you will handle an article, story, or book, you are solving two reading problems with one approach.

CHAPTER VIII

STEP FOUR:

Build Your Vocabulary!

Some years ago, an employee of a prominent advertising agency saved his job by creating one of the most popular television commercials in history. Below is an excerpt from a magazine article analyzing the extraordinary success of the ad.

Read the selection with every effort aimed at full comprehension. If you have difficulty with some of the words, don't stop to think about them. Keep going at a good speed and then take the test that follows. There will be one set of questions you haven't tried before.

Having saved his job, the young man is probably sojourning in French Morocco by now, or some equally exotic resort, with lots of flowers, expensive cigars, and quite possibly a couple of enchanting local denizens draped attractively on his arm. He could also be contemplating accepting the vice-presidency those "wonderful chaps" at the agency have been thrusting under his nose or perhaps he is deciding to continue to soak up some more of that transoceanic culture.

The point is, his is one of those enviable success stories that are based on a facile imagination, incisive action, and an acute awareness of what the public (a very ambiguous term) enjoys these days in the way of ads. John Doe's opinions change as erratically and as often as the products that beckon to him. As many bitter ad men are realizing, it is as necessary to keep abreast of new advertising methods as it is of technical progress in industry. Both are equally vital in sales appeal.

Our bright young man knew the sacred trinity of achieving his mission. First, and most fundamental, he employed the idea of avoiding mundane imitation and, instead, used an entirely new and refreshing approach. Secondly, he kept the contents of the ad within the confines of a simple layout and devoid of prodigious copy. Third, and to my mind the genius of good advertising, he threw in copious quantities of good old American humor. These three concepts are basic in the creation of appealing advertisements.

COMPREHENSION TEST

(Place a ✔ before the answer of your choice.)

A. Main ideas and details

1. A good title for this selection would be

_____ a. Traveling Abroad

_____ b. Writing Successful Ads

_____ c. A Bright Young Man

2. The creator of the ad

_____ a. left to live abroad

_____ b. resigned

_____ c. was offered a promotion

3. Success of an ad depends heavily on

   _____ a. guessing public reaction
   _____ b. writing sophisticated copy
   _____ c. limiting the humor

B. Other features

1. The writer's purpose was to

   _____ a. solicit customers
   _____ b. defend the young man
   _____ c. suggest how to create successful ads

2. His point of view was

   _____ a. pleasantly informative
   _____ b. quite matter of fact
   _____ c. highly sarcastic

3. His style featured careful word-choice to

   _____ a. establish reliability
   _____ b. develop sharp and clear meaning
   _____ c. stress his superiority of judgment

4. The hidden meaning in the article is that, in the world of advertising, one

   _____ a. produces or gets out
   _____ b. can see the world
   _____ c. can have a lot of fun

C. Selected vocabulary

Here are 12 words that appeared in the selection. Place a ✔ before the correct definitions.

1. *sojourning*	visiting	working	living permanently
2. *exotic*	domestic	southern	foreign
3. *denizens*	females	inhabitants	capes
4. *facile*	heavy	skillful	foolish
5. *incisive*	sharp	dull	dental
6. *acute*	pretty	keen	long
7. *ambiguous*	harsh	two-handed	unclear
8. *erratically*	falsely	unpredictably	frequently
9. *trinity*	set of three	holy place	belief
10. *mundane*	ordinary	weekly	striking
11. *prodigious*	childish	wise	huge
12. *copious*	sparing	abundant	clever

ANSWERS: A.   1-b, 2-c, 3-a   B.   1-c, 2-a, 3-b, 4-a
             C.   1-visiting, 2-foreign, 3-inhabitants,
                  4-skillful, 5-sharp, 6-keen, 7-unclear,
                  8-unpredictably, 9-set of three,
                  10-ordinary, 11-huge, 12-abundant

Did you score 100% in both the comprehension and vocabulary tests? If you did, you need not be too concerned about building up your reading vocabulary because it already is above average. You will perhaps want to browse through the remainder of this chapter to see whether you can make a few valuable additions to your present stock of words.

On the other hand, if you are like most readers who are trying to improve, you had considerable difficulty with some of the words. And yet you probably were able to answer the comprehension questions correctly. How was it possible for you to reach a good understanding of what you were reading even though you did not know the meanings of a half dozen or more words?

For one thing, you were able to grasp the central point the writer made because you are familiar with the subject matter. It is impossible for anyone to escape the impact of advertising these days. Your own experience, therefore, enabled you to bring considerable knowledge to the article.

Secondly, you very likely did what most readers unconsciously do, or should do, when they come across unfamiliar words. They work out acceptable meanings from the context. For example, *French Morocco* surely gave you good clues to the meanings of both *sojourning* and *exotic*. Similarly, *local* and *attractively* certainly suggest that our young man must have become acquainted with some of the good-looking women of the area. Again, the way *facile, incisive,* and *acute* are attached to key words in the sentence implies something good, and that's close enough to carry the thought.

It should not be surprising, then, that a reader can understand a passage even when he can't give precise definitions for as many as 5% of the words on a page. You have been told before that, if difficult words are sufficiently scattered in a selection, they need not seriously impair your ability to comprehend main ideas and important details, provided you keep moving and set your sights on the broad values of the contents. But, you say, if you do understand what you are reading, what difference does it make whether you know all the words or not?

Let's look at it this way. You listen to some fine music and enjoy yourself immensely because it is tuneful and puts you into a favorable mood. Or you examine a painting and like the scene or the way the people look, and are impressed with the richness of the colors. You understand a little here, appreciate a little there, but you are secretly bothered that others are getting much more out of the same thing. You wonder whether you wouldn't more actively follow what the composer was trying to say if you had some knowledge of musical composition. You ask yourself whether the painting wouldn't have deeper meaning for you if you understood why the artist used a particular technique, what determined his choice of pigments, and why he placed certain objects or figures where he did on the canvas. In short, you feel like a person with a heavy cold who is eating a delicious-looking dinner, can identify every dish, but cannot taste very much.

This brings us back to our words. If your only objective in reading were to get main ideas and a few details out of the average article or book, you could probably do quite satisfactorily when you didn't encounter too many strange words. But you must be convinced by now that comprehension means much more than merely the surface interpretation. Since it does, how else are you to get to the personality and depth of a piece of writing except through the author's words? They are as necessary to him as notes are to the composer, paints and brushes to the artist. You can no more fully appreciate what you read without a solid vocabulary background than you can any of the arts without some knowledge of the materials and techniques involved.

The more words you are familiar with in a selection, the greater your comprehension is and the easier it is for you to look for the keys to understanding and appreciation. You should not be satisfied with a blurred picture of meaning. A rich vocabulary is your best device for bringing it into sharp and clear focus.

"But," you say, "haven't I been repeatedly told to concentrate on groups of words and not to worry about individual words, if I wish to avoid being a slow and confused word-by-word reader?"

Yes, you have been told quite emphatically to STRETCH YOUR SPAN. Nor is there any intention here to change this advice. However, it is once more a matter of *how much meaning* you get out of each word phrase. Take the following sentence from our first selection:

144

The young man is *probably sojourning* in French Morocco by now, or some other *equally exotic resort,* with lots of flowers, expensive cigars, and quite possibly a couple of *enchanting local denizens* draped attractively on his arm.

If you read it properly, you permitted your eyes to stop no more than two or three times across a line. We will assume that you were able to get the thought of the sentence—the young man is probably in some faraway place and is having a good time. But notice the phrases in italics. Suppose you didn't know any of the three key words involved. You could still handle each of the word groups in single recognition spans without loss of speed or understanding of the central thought. However, wouldn't you wonder what one does when he "sojourns," whether an "exotic" resort is good or bad, and what kind of women "denizens" are?

No, you are not suddenly being told that you must start concentrating on one word at a time in a line of print. Indeed not! You *are* being told that an increase in your vocabulary will make what you include in your recognition spans so much more interesting and meaningful.

Further evidence that word study is not a contradiction of phrase-by-phrase reading is that almost all standardized tests that measure reading ability contain not only questions in paragraph interpretation but also in word recognition. What's more, results on such examinations usually show remarkable similarity in the areas tested. Readers who do poorly with the paragraphs perform just as poorly in the vocabulary section. A few pages back you read of the "sacred trinity" of advertising. Reading has one of its own: rate, comprehension, and vocabulary. They are so interdependent that unless progress is made in all three it is difficult to make progress in any one of them.

This is how rate fits into the picture. No matter how quickly you may try to read a selection that has many unfamiliar words, you will be slowed up considerably because of the numerous blanks that appear in the images you send to your mind. These continual frustrations you experience in your efforts at rapid comprehension necessarily affect your confidence and skill. You find yourself submitting to regressions, perhaps, because you feel compelled to take a second look at a word, or you may unconsciously try saying the word aloud to help you understand it, or, what is worst of all, you keep jumping from book to dictionary and then back again. There seems to be no end to the problems a limited vocabulary can create: more roadblocks, narrower recognition span, lower speed, and inadequate comprehension.

*   *   *

If you had twenty years of leisure time ahead of you and you could devote at least 3 or 4 hours a day to reading, I would be able to suggest *the best way* to increase your vocabulary. My advice would simply be—*read*. Read anything and everything. Read newspapers, magazines, books, pamphlets—poems, essays, short stories, novels, plays, biographies, textbooks. With all this reading you would be exposed to new words over and over again. The context alone would be sufficient to establish your familiarity with them. Many would rapidly become part of your recognition vocabulary, and eventually you would include the formerly strange words in your speech and writing activities.

This, by the way, is how you learned most of the words you use today. As a child, between the ages of two and six, you picked up one word at a time by listening and looking. No one gave you a list of words to study. In the lower grades of school you added many more words as the result of wider experiences and a few at the direction of the teacher. Certainly as your education proceeded, you had increasing amounts of direct word study, but most of your vocabulary improvement occurred in an indirect way.

It would be a mistake for me to tell you to read extensively and let your vocabulary take care of itself. Beyond a doubt, that would be best. But let's face it. You just can't or haven't the time to do it that way. Even if you had a great deal of leisure, you couldn't increase your reading program drastically through sheer will power alone. Human nature is against it. You resist being pushed into activities you don't do well.

When you learn to read faster and comprehend better, you will want to read more. You won't have to be urged to do so. In the long run you will get into the cycle of wider reading bringing about a better vocabulary and *vice versa*. But in the early stages of your training, you will have to settle for the second-best method of acquiring new words. That is to study them directly.

Remember, it was one of the methods used to help you learn to read in school and it's a perfectly valid device today. It will quicken your interest in words, prove to you that you *can* increase your vocabulary, and set the stage for the improvement that will come as the result of frequent and varied reading without special study.

Our aim in the rest of this chapter is to show you how to master an average of 20 words a month, *a rate that will be 10 times faster than your present one!* The system was successfully developed after years of experimentation with evening adult classes at New York University. The students range in background from those with one or two years of high school education to others with professional degrees. We cover from 6 to 10 new words a week. At the end of the semester (5 months), the group consistently averages well over 90% retention.

These are busy people. Most of them have full-time jobs. Many are married and have families. Yet they manage to spend the few minutes a day to master their assignments. What is most gratifying is that after a while they become word-conscious. They report a thrill of recognition when they find some of their favorites in the things they read and hear. They tell stories of valiant efforts to impress friends and associates with newborn vocabulary skill. When they reach this point, there is no further concern about their progress. It is clear that they will get there!

You can get there, too. But you are going to take a somewhat different road. You will follow the same system used in the classes, with one important difference.

In dealing with a group of 25 to 35 adults, it becomes necessary to work with some sort of list of words. It is more efficient to use uniform material when varied backgrounds and abilities are merged. Accordingly, we set up lists by having students contribute words they have become interested in during a given week. The words to be studied are determined by the frequency with which each appears in the student contributions.

Since you have accepted the responsibility of studying by yourself, you should not become dependent upon a list. On an individual basis, such an approach is not advisable because there are important limitations on the value of any list not developed by you, suited to your needs and abilities. Consider how most vocabulary lists are prepared.

A careful and extended survey is made of representative newspapers, magazines, books, pamphlets, speeches, television and radio programs, motion pictures, and existing vocabulary manuals and research reports. Then a table of frequency is established; that is, an actual count

148

is taken of the number of times particular words appear in the samplings. In this way, the words are graded as to difficulty in terms of age level and school placement. Finally, lists emerge, each supposedly suitable for special groups beginning with the lower elementary grades up to the "educated adult."

Unfortunately, any one list has the same disadvantages as do all. Someone else chose the reading materials from which the words were selected, *not you!* That someone may have guessed wrong in deciding what *you* normally read or hear. Many words on an artificial list may already be known to you, especially if the estimates of your tastes were too low. Or words may have been picked that you would never use, see rarely, or simply do not want to bother learning.

It is an established law of learning that best results are obtained when the materials selected for attention arise out of the needs of the students. In short, if *you* pick the words, you are more likely to be interested in studying them because the need to do so has come out of your own experience. Your aim will be neither too high nor too low. The collector of a list may have left out many words that he concluded were too easy for you. Consequently, hundreds of words that you may need to study first are omitted and you struggle with others that are too much for you at the moment. To avoid being discouraged by what seems like an unattainable goal, you must spend your time on words that are suited to your immediate reading, social, and professional interests.

It is for these reasons that the vocabulary-building program soon to be described will be based upon words of your own choosing. We won't waste time on nonsense like "300 Words Every Person Should Know"! You will make all the decisions about what words you think you should know. And now, you are ready to learn how to become your own list-maker.

VOCABULARY PLAN

There are four steps. Each will be explained and illustrated. Read through all the instructions first, so that you become familiar with the mechanics of the plan before you do independent work.

I. Choosing the Words

"When I read I keep a dictionary at my side. As soon as I come to a word I don't know, I look it up right away. Then I go on reading."

You've heard people say this, or perhaps you've used this method yourself because you thought it was a good way to learn words. Well, it's not—for several reasons!

Stop-and-go reading destroys the continuity you must maintain if you are to achieve full comprehension. Your primary objective is to get the author's ideas quickly and to enjoy the other features of his writing. You can't do that if you interrupt yourself every minute to look up the meaning of a word.

Secondly, it has been demonstrated to you how the context can give you enough information about strange words to enable you to continue reading without stopping. To refresh your memory, we'll review the process by taking an excerpt from a newspaper article:

If the women of Kabul had the vote, the chances are that the *chadri* would quickly vanish from Afghanistan's capital.

When your mind registered *Kabul*, it probably vaguely wondered where it was. And when it spotted *chadri*, it was definitely stopped. However, by the end of the sentence your problem about the location of the city was already solved. Observe what happened if you moved right along to the next sentence:

But as matters stand, the chadri, also known as the burka, still envelops the Moslem female population here.

By this time you can guess that *chadri* and *burka* refer to some sort of garment because of the presence of *envelops*. Let's say you continued to the next two sentences:

The hooded robes banish them from view and virtually shut out the sun. Eyeholes are provided to give the women a peek at the outside world and enable them to maneuver about.

Is there any further doubt about the meaning of *chadri* or *burka?* The same sort of thing usually happens when you read material written by skilled writers. They know it is their responsibility to make the meanings of uncommon words clear without forcing you to run to a dictionary.

There is another inescapable fact that speaks against what I call word-hopping. An unabridged dictionary of the English language contains more than 600,000 entries. Certainly no one can expect to learn more than a small fraction of this enormous quantity in one lifetime. Indeed, very few of those remarkable people who seem to know any word that comes up have a vocabulary that even approaches 20 per cent of the grand total. This fact indicates *why* it is a waste of time to try to learn every word you see and *how important it is that you choose the right ones to study*.

Before you make any choice, you must decide what use

you want to make of the word. Actually, you have four vocabularies. The largest is the one you bring to your **silent reading.** Here you have at your disposal not only the words you feel capable of using in speech and writing, but also many more that you have learned to recognize in context. The latter group is very much part of your vocabulary, but it does not play an active role.

Somewhat smaller is your **listening** vocabulary. Because you must absorb the material as fast as the speaker talks, you lose the meanings of some of the words you would ordinarily recognize in printed form. Your ability to recall is less effective when you hear than when you see.

Going down the scale, we come next to your **writing** vocabulary. Experience has taught you that you must know a word thoroughly before you can safely include it in a sentence. A rough idea is not enough because failure to pick the right form or meaning in a given situation can prove to be very embarrassing. For instance, an individual hears and sees combinations like *"condign* punishment" or *"condign* reward." He guesses rightly that the word means "well-deserved, worthy." How distressing it must be to him, however, if someone calls his attention to the mistake he has made when he writes (as one of my students once did):

"The rascal *condigned* everything that was done to him."

The fact that the word had no verb form had never occurred to him. To avoid such situations, most people tend to leave out a good percentage of their vocabulary when they write, and so they use far fewer words than they can recognize.

Your weakest is your **speaking** vocabulary. Here again the time factor is significant. Your words must come out at a reasonably rapid rate to avoid giving the impression that you are fumbling. Hence, you discard a great many words that you know well enough to write with and many more that have meaning for you when you read or listen.

Your objectives in vocabulary study, then, should be threefold:

1. Not to allow it to interfere with your rate and comprehension.
2. To use the context of the material you read to add words to your recognition vocabulary so that your reading and listening experiences become more meaningful.
3. Through study and practice, to gradually move more words into your "use" vocabulary. You have really learned a word when *by your own choice* you use it correctly and comfortably in writing or speaking.

With this information in mind, you can establish a regular pattern of selecting words for study. Whenever possible during reading sessions, keep a pencil and a pad of paper at your side. Draw a line down the center of each page so that you have two blank columns. How you use the pad will be explained in a moment, but there is one more job to be done. In your notebook, set up a Vocabulary Chart divided thus:

Word	Pronunciation	Meanings	Forms	Original Sentence	My Sentences

You will need two pages across to allow enough space for the entries. For the time being, we'll concern ourselves with the entries in only the first column.

You are now ready with two of the tools you will need to handle the unusual words you are likely to encounter in any one reading session. You treat such words very much the same way you do people you meet.

There are some you are introduced to for the first time at large gatherings. You nod politely, undoubtedly forget their names five minutes later, and possibly never see them again. Similarly, in the average column or page you may come upon a word or two that you have never seen before, which can be classified as a chance acquaintance. A word like *chadri* would fall into this category. You do the best you can to identify its meaning from the contents, and that's all. You may or may not recognize it a second time, but you make no special effort to retain it. If it becomes part of your recognition vocabulary, good. If not, you haven't lost much.

Then there are those people whom you see two or three times at various places. In time you reach the point where you make a conscious effort to remember their names, but you haven't exchanged home visits yet. They are acquaintances, not friends. They are like the words that begin to look familiar to you after you have come across them in your reading *several times.* You are certain you will meet them again, and you decide that you should begin to know them a little better so that they will at least become part of your reading and listening vocabularies. With such words, you do this:

1. As you read, note the number of the page on which the word appeared and jot it down in the *left-hand column*

on your pad. Learn to do this mechanically so that it does not cause you to remove your eyes from the material.

2. When you have finished your reading, go back to the pages noted and find the words you thought you wanted to look at again. This way you avoid interruptions, you get valuable training in skimming (see Chapter XI), and you have time to determine which of the words you have selected should constitute the group that will get a second look. Don't be too ambitious. About two or three such words are enough for one sitting. Then you:

a. Look at the word again.
b. Guess at the meaning again by reviewing the context and using the techniques that will shortly be described.
c. Check the meaning and pronunciation with a dictionary.
d. Say the word aloud.
e. That's all! *You do not enter these words in your notebook yet.*

Finally, we come to those words you have met often enough to convince you that you ought to begin treating them like friends, like the people you know intimately and expect to see regularly in your social activities. For the sake of providing you with a definite yardstick, let's say you have come across these words at least a half dozen times in your reading and have *heard* them used by speakers whose cultural background you respect. This is the group you should study seriously:

1. As you read, jot down in the *right-hand column* of your pad the page numbers on which the words appear. You are going to move them up from your recognition to your "use" vocabulary. They will soon make their way into your speech and writing.

2. Enter the words in the first column of your Vocabulary Chart. Make certain you get the spellings correct.

3. Number the entries from 1 to 5. When you have accumulated 5 words, you have a 1-week study unit.

4. Put your notebook aside. Once you have started a program of this kind, you will always be in the midst of word-study units. You take each group of 5 in its turn. You need not study a particular word on the spot. There is no hurry. The words have been around for years. They'll still be there even if it takes you a few months to catch up with them. There is no sense deluding yourself. You won't become vocabulary-rich in a week, ten days, or a month. It is a process that takes time, but the rewards are so worthwhile that there can be no question about the desirability of expending the effort.

II. Studying the Words

A. HOW TO GUESS INTELLIGENTLY

Since you need not include a word in a study unit until you have seen and heard it used more than a half dozen times, you will be depending mainly upon your ability to guess at its meaning so long as it remains a part of only your recognition vocabulary. True, you will check with a dictionary now and then, but you must have found out by now that definitions have a habit of eluding you shortly after you have looked up a word. Therefore, it is sensible for you to reduce the probabilities of developing the wrong idea of a word by perfecting various techniques that can serve as your "guessing dictionary."

1. Context

You have already had several examples of how to use the context of a selection to work out the meaning of a strange word. The point to stress here is that you must not get panicky if the sentence in which the word first appears does not give you enough of a hint to enable you to guess reasonably accurately. The sentences that follow usually add more to the meaning, assuming that the material has been skillfully written. Therefore, you must keep moving right through the paragraph and try to pick up more information about the word as you read further.

There is one caution. If you begin reading something that has about 15 or 20 words per page that are entirely new to you, I would suggest that you lay the material aside. You very likely aren't ready for it. It is unwise to jump in over your head. Try again when your vocabulary is stronger.

2. Breaking words down

Like most living things that grow larger and heavier as they get older, languages gain lengthier and more complicated words as they mature. This is not to say that all short words are simple in meaning, but the bulk of your "difficult" words contain more than two syllables. In many instances, this stretching process has occurred by the addition of "pieces" before or after the original easily understood monosyllable (one syllable), thus forming a polysyllable (more than one syllable).

English is no exception to this language process and has its full share of polysyllables, many of which seem to be difficult by virtue of their length. However, if you train yourself to become familiar with some of the more common "pieces" that are added, you will possess a second guessing device that will unravel the meanings of a surprisingly large number of words.

For example, we can start with a monosyllable like *port,* which came from the Latin *porto,* meaning *to carry.* Note how it can be built up:

*ex*port	to carry out
*im*port	to carry in
port*able*	able to be carried
port*er*	one who carries
*trans*port*ation*	that which carries or means of carrying across or from one place to another

There is no limit to the number of "pieces" that can be added at the beginning or end of a shorter word. A well-known monstrosity can be traced to the Latin *sto,* meaning *to stand.* It wasn't enough to put *en* (in) in front and *able* (able to) and *ish* (to make) at the end, thus forming the word *establish,* meaning literally *to make able to stand.* Look what happened to the word by the time some others got through with it:

*dis*establish	*to break up* the ability to stand
*anti*disestablish	*against* the above
antidisestablish*ment*	*that which* is against breaking up the ability to stand
antidisestablishment*arian*	*one who* favors that which is against breaking up the ability to stand
antidisestablishmentarian*ism*	*system or belief* of those who are against breaking up the ability to stand

Actually, the word was formed to express the opposition of certain groups to the separation of church from state.

Fortunately, very few words get out of hand this way. Rarely are more than four or five syllables used. You can see, however, that when it is broken down, the long word is not nearly as formidable as it seemed.

158

These "pieces" that we have been talking about are called:

Prefixes   *Pre* (before, in front of)
            fix (to fasten)
Suffixes   *Suf* (from *sub,* under)
            fix (to fasten)
            (Since we cannot fasten *under* a word, the word has come to mean that which is attached after.)
Roots   These are the forms that function exactly as the word implies. When prefixes and suffixes are added to roots, words grow in size.

Before giving you a list of the more common "pieces," let me advise you not to try to memorize them. The object is to get into the habit of looking for them when you are guessing and to become increasingly familiar with them as you learn to break words down. You will discover that you will remember most prefixes, suffixes, and roots after you have consciously identified them for a time in your dictionary work.

Another point to bear in mind is that English words, like those in other languages, are subject to what is called *assimilation*. This comes about as the result of the normal human habit of adjusting things so that they are easier to say or do. For instance, *affix* comes from *ad* (to) and *fix* (to attach or fasten). However, people found it difficult to say *adfix,* and so gradually those who spoke the word assimilated the *d* into the *f* that followed, thus giving us *affix*. Sometimes, instead of assimilating one letter into another, speakers simply dropped the offending one, and we have a word like *amend* developing from a*d*mend.

The curious influence of speech upon spelling is most often found in the prefixes. Therefore, you must be alert to the effects of assimilation as you break down words:

TYPICAL EXAMPLE

Prefix AD

*ac*commodate	*am*munition
*af*fluent	*an*nex
*ag*gregate	*ap*ply
*a*kin	*ar*rest
*al*ly	*as*sist
*a*mass	*at*tack

a. Common prefixes

ab	from	*ab*normal	*in*	not	*in*capable
ad	to toward	*ad*mit	*ex*	out	*ex*it
			per	through	*per*ceive
be	by	*be*side	*pre*	before	*pre*pare
bi	two	*bi*sect	*pro*	in front for	*pro*hibit *pro*noun
com,		*com*pose			
con	with	*con*nect	*re*	back	*re*mit
con	against	*con*test	*sub*	under	*sub*tract
de	from	*de*tract	*super*	over, above	*super*vise
dis	apart	*dis*miss	*trans*	across	*trans*port
en, in	in	*en*trance *in*sert	*un*	not	*un*fit

b. Common suffixes

able, ible	able to	lik*able*, admiss*ible*
age	act or process, relationship, place of abode, fee	marri*age*, shrink*age*, orphan*age*, tow*age*
al, ial	pertaining to, like	loc*al*, best*ial*
ance, ence	act of, state or condition	assist*ance*, viol*ence*
ant, ent	one who, that which	serv*ant*, lat*ent*
ary, ery	that which, relation to, one who, place, act	station*ary*, diet*ary*, no*tary*, bak*ery*, arch*ery*

ate	characterized by or caused to	desol*ate*, fascin*ate*
ful	full of, containing	taste*ful*, beauti*ful*
ice	act, quality, condition	serv*ice*, apprent*ice*
ine, in	characterized by, name of	sal*ine*, chlor*ine*, gas-ol*ine*, maudl*in*
ion, sion, tion	act or result of, condition	un*ion*, eva*sion*, sta*tion*
ist	one who	violin*ist*
ive	quality of or tending to	act*ive*, conclus*ive*
ment	state, quality, condition	amaze*ment*, judg*ment*
or, er	one who, that which	act*or*, raz*or*, writ*er*
ous, ious	full of, like, having qualities of	fam*ous*, bulb*ous*, poison*ous*, deli*cious*
ure	act or process, being, result of	expos*ure*, legisla*ture*, pict*ure*

Suffixes usually do not cause changes of meanings in words as do prefixes. As you have gathered by now, most of the suffixes help to create people or things, describe them, or compare them. Another way of saying this is that these word endings help form the various parts of speech:

Noun	right
Verb	right
Adjectives	righteous, rightful
Adverbs	righteously, rightfully

c. Common roots

The roots are the most important "pieces" since they are the sources of the basic and extended meanings of words. Most roots come from the French and Latin importations, as well as the ancestor of our language, Anglo-

161

Saxon, although we have also borrowed liberally from the rest of the world. Again, it would be silly to try to memorize the thousands of roots in English, but it is a good idea to become familiar with the more common ones because they help you not only in working out new words but in discovering a deeper meaning in words you thought you already knew.

mote	move	*motion, promote, emote, emotion, demote*
jur	swear	*conjure, jury, abjure, perjury*
serve	guard or serve	*service, disservice, servant, serviceable, deserve, conserve, preserve*
solv	loose, free	*solve, dissolve, resolve, absolve, insoluble*
vent	come	*event, advent, convent, invent, prevent*
ject	throw	*project, projectile, abject, adjective, dejection, projection*
tend	stretch	*attend, pretend, contend, distend, superintendent, intend*
vert	turn	*convert, avert, divert, invert, revert, subversion*
gen	born	*genial, generation, congenial, gender, generous, generate, genocide*
greg	flock, group	*gregarious, congregate, segregate, aggregate, congregation*
pend	hang	*pendant, depend, append, expend, suspend*
scribe	write	*describe, inscribe, ascribe, conscription, prescribe, subscribe*
spect	look	*inspect, aspect, spectacle, spectacular, respect, suspect*
terr	earth	*terrace, terra cotta (cooked), terrain, territory*

Being able to break down words into their roots plus their suffixes and prefixes is an invaluable aid in your eventual mastery of a word as well as in your early efforts to guess its meaning. If you met *introversion* for the first time and knew some of the common "pieces," you could so easily come up with an acceptable interpretation:

intro	in, inward
vers (from *vert*)	to turn
ion	act of

(act of turning inward, being withdrawn in personality)

Certainly if you decided to study the word so that you could use it, you would have established a firm foundation upon which to build a permanent addition to your vocabulary.

In general, when you are trying to break down a word, attack the root first, then go on to the prefix, and finally to the suffix. You can practice doing this by going back to the sample words offered after the list of roots and testing your skill with those words that are not very familiar to you and then checking your results with a dictionary. It can become a fascinating game, and it is a wonderful way to observe the logic that exists in language structure and the simplicity that underlies even the most difficult words. It is a never-ending thrill for me to come across a word like *arenaceous*, for example, look for and find *arena* in it, and with the help of the context, decide that the word must mean *sandy* because arenas were originally sandy areas for various activities and games. Or, the first time I came across *disingenuous*, I saw *gen* in the middle, knew it came from the Latin "to give birth, to be born," and proceeded from there. The prefix *in* told me that *ingenuous* meant "state at birth" or "innocent, open, frank." But the addition of *dis (apart from* or *without)* turned the meaning of the word around to "insincere, false, artificial." In each instance, when the dictionary confirmed my guesses, I felt like a Sherlock Holmes among words.

3. Word families

This third technique, designed to help you guess intelligently, can often solve your problem of what to do about a word whose root seems foreign to you because it is not one of those you have worked with often enough to know at a glance. Let's say you come across *apathetic*. You can guess that the root is probably *path,* but it isn't on the list of roots you have learned. Your next step is to try to think of a word you do know that contains the same root. *Sympathy* readily comes to mind. In this word, *path* rather obviously refers to *feeling* or *emotion*. Once you have come this far, you turn to the prefix *a,* which you know means *from* or *away*. The logical conclusion, then, is that *apathetic* refers to the absence of feeling.

Many words come in families, and often by identifying one word you can become acquainted with all the relatives. With the above information, for example, you could do something with:

pathos   apathy

empathy   pathetic

antipathy

Sample sentences

There was great *pathos* in the story, and handkerchiefs were freely used by the audience.

The new play was greeted with considerable *apathy* by the critics, and it closed in a week.

164

Watching little children at play stirs an *empathy* in people who recall their own carefree days.

The *pathetic* look on his face brought many coins into his box.

His *antipathy* for formality accounted for his wardrobe of slacks and casual jackets.

Now try your skill in the following exercises based on word families.

1. *Chili con carne* consists of red peppers with *meat.*

   The *carnage* of battle produces

   _____ a. great glory
   _____ b. broken bodies

   Carnal pleasures are those of

   _____ a. the mind
   _____ b. the flesh

   Belief in *reincarnation* includes the expectation of a return as

   _____ a. a live person
   _____ b. a ghost

   The *carnation's* original color was

   _____ a. red
   _____ b. white

   A *carnivorous* animal eats

   _____ a. vegetables
   _____ b. other animals

2. If someone gives you *credit,* he *believes* you will pay.

An *incredible* story is

____ a. very factual
____ b. a pack of lies

A *credulous* person can

____ a. be told anything
____ b. see through you

My *credo* is part of my

____ a. conscience
____ b. information

If I place *credence* in your statement, I

____ a. want more evidence
____ b. accept it

3. A *courier* is a *runner* or messenger, and *current* events are *going on now*.

When he *incurred* a debt, he

____ a. paid it
____ b. assumed it

Recurrent attacks are those that

____ a. keep coming back
____ b. stop

Cursory reading is

____ a. very slow
____ b. very fast

When people *concur,* they

____ a. agree
____ b. disagree

Precursory events bring us

_____ a. confusion
_____ b. hints

An *incursion* on my rights reflects

_____ a. invasion
_____ b. cooperation

4. I *comprehend* because I actually *seize* the meaning.

The *prehensile* tail of the monkey helps him

_____ a. grab branches
_____ b. swat flies

I am *apprehensive* if I feel my heart

_____ a. jump with joy
_____ b. pound with fear

When a person is *apprehended,* he is

_____ a. caught
_____ b. released

A *reprehensible* deed is

_____ a. praiseworthy
_____ b. blameworthy

5. The *medieval* period is also called the *Middle* Ages.

Mediocre talents are

_____ a. unusual
_____ b. ordinary

An *intermediary* is a person who

____ a. starts an argument
____ b. settles one

A *mediator*

____ a. takes sides
____ b. sits between opponents

A *median* in a set of figures occurs

____ a. at the beginning
____ b. halfway down

A *medium* claims her mind floats

____ a. between heaven and earth
____ b. along the surface of the earth

If you were able to handle the exercises just concluded without too much trouble, you became familiar with a group of thirty words that are above average in difficulty. Together with the words you picked up when you practiced with the common roots and their families, you added an astonishingly large number of new words to your recognition vocabulary in a short space of time. Make it a habit when you look up a word in a dictionary to find its root. Then think of various prefixes and suffixes that might be added to it, and browse through the pages to discover whether you have come across another word family. When you have become expert at doing this, not only will you learn many new words but you will be fascinated by the interesting possibilities that exist in word study.

B. USING THE DICTIONARY

You will, of course, need a dictionary to help you in

your vocabulary work. Make sure yours is a good one. Here are some features it should have:

1. Pronunciation

The symbols used to indicate vowel and consonant sounds should be easily followed and illustrated by sample words. In addition, the pronunciation key should be repeated at the top or bottom of *every page*. You should not be annoyed by being forced to refer to the front of the book when you want to figure out how to say a word.

There should also be a guide to pronunciation in the opening portions of the dictionary to explain the symbols used and to give some general rules about their application. The appendix should include special sections devoted to the pronunciation of places and names.

2. Etymology

This refers to the origin or derivation of a word in terms of its basic root, prefix, and language ancestry. Such information should be supplied so that you can identify word families, gain increasing familiarity with word parts, and enjoy the fun of seeing how a language develops. Some dictionaries either leave out the etymology or insert it only now and then.

Very often a look at the etymology of a word will set its meaning in your mind permanently. You obtain a *clue*, so to speak, that doesn't easily escape you because the unusual nature of the information may help you retain it in the same manner as you tend to remember odd and silly things better than you do logical or factual ones. Suppose, for example, you look up *supercilious* and learn that it breaks down into *raised (super)* and *eyebrow* or *eyelid (cilium)*. You now have a picture in your mind of the expression on a person's face when he is attempting

169

to act superior. Certainly knowing this forms a stronger bond for you between the word and its meaning than the definition alone.

Or you learn that *debonair* is derived from *of (de)*, *good (bon)*, and *type* or *class (aire)*. Besides now knowing that the word means *courteous* or *graceful*, you also have a strong clue to help you uncover its meaning when you meet it again. It is for such purposes that you should make sure your dictionary has ample etymological information.

3. Sample phrases or sentences

Each unusual word should be illustrated by a phrase or sentence so that you will not be studying the meaning in isolation. You can compare this usage with the way the word was used in the sentence in which you found it. Also, these examples help you develop proficiency in using the various forms of the word—noun, adjective, verb, etc.

4. Illustrations

There should be pictures, diagrams, and sketches whenever these seem necessary to support the definition. Although the expression "One picture is worth a thousand words" is not always true, it very frequently is in a dictionary, especially in connection with technical and scientific terms.

5. Synonyms

Sufficient synonyms should be provided so that you can use your dictionary not only to get a definition but also to substitute a word for the original if you should desire to avoid repetition. Moreover, a synonym, too, will sometimes help you remember the meaning of a word.

For instance, *inebriate* is a more polite way of referring to a drunk. The oddity of so imposing a word meaning what it does may in itself influence you to use it more often and thus strengthen your recollection of its definition.

6. Varied meanings

Good dictionaries number the meanings of a word that is used under varying conditions. Usually, the first definition is the most common and the ones that follow are specialized in nature. A simple word like *dog,* besides its obvious meaning, also refers colloquially to "a rascally fellow," astronomically to a star cluster, mechanically to a type of fastening used in logging, and meteorologically to a "sundog, fogdog," etc. Unless all the meanings of a particular word are in your dictionary, you may not find the one that suits the sentence you are trying to comprehend. It is very important to avoid forming a completely false idea of how a word is generally used when you first meet it.

7. Spelling

Common spelling rules should be listed, generally in the introductory portions, so that you can learn how to handle large groups of words. Look up the *accented-syllable rule* sometime and see how it will solve for you the spellings of thousands of words that may have given you trouble before. What is just as important is that good spelling habits are extremely important to vocabulary development. You have been told that you really know a word when you use it voluntarily in your writing. If lack of confidence about the spelling of certain words prevents you from using them, you can see how long it will take you to make them part of your "use" vocabulary.

8. Abbreviations

You will want to use these occasionally when you write, and you should be able to find them in the same book you use for definitions.

9. Proper nouns

Any noun that is spelled with a capital letter is a proper noun—a name of a person, place, or thing. Such entries should be in the text of the dictionary; other proper nouns should be found in the special sections reserved for giving you the pronunciation of well-known people and places. If you can look up *Colosseum,* for example, you can find out how it is said, the fact that it was an amphitheater built in about 80 A.D., and that the name came from *colossus* (gigantic), a term also used to name one of the Seven Wonders of the World. Such information makes a dictionary a biographical, geographical, and historical treasure chest.

10. Punctuation

The rules for punctuation should be listed in a special section. This will help make your dictionary a complete writing instrument.

When you consider how much useful information can be found in a good dictionary, you can understand why it is unwise to short-change yourself. Get one that can do the job for you. Don't use an inferior tool.

*   *   *

We are now ready for the instructions in the use of a dictionary to help you study words. For this purpose we return to our Vocabulary Chart. A description of how to make each entry follows. Since we have already discussed in detail how to choose a word for Column 1, we continue with:

Column 2—Pronunciation

Enter the word as the dictionary has it, with the vowel symbols and accent mark. In words of four or more syllables, you may find two accent marks: a primary (heavy) and a secondary (light) stress. Note that when the pronunciation is shown the spelling is frequently altered to accommodate the sounds. Column 1, of course, is the official spelling.

Should you have trouble determining whether you are accenting the syllable indicated, try this simple device. Cut a strip of paper, about an inch wide and six or seven inches long, from a newspaper. When you are about to say a word, hold the strip vertically in front of and about an inch away from your lips. Exaggerate the force of air you expel as you accent the syllable called for in the pronunciation breakdown. If the strip jumps back at the proper syllable, you have accented the word correctly. If it moves as you hit some other syllable or doesn't jump at all, you will have to try again. Of course, you don't exaggerate the pronunciation once you have the accent well in hand.

Column 3—Meanings

Jot down the common meanings, and a few synonyms. Do not bother with the specialized definitions unless you are particularly interested or you think you will have use for them. If your study of the etymology turns up a word family or provides you with an unusual clue to the meaning, write that in, too. In the latter case, underline the entry so that it stands out when you review.

Column 4—Forms

Insert the various parts of speech into which the word can be formed. In some instances it might be necessary to enter a negative phrase as a warning; for example, *condign—not as a verb.*

Column 5—Original sentence (facing page of notebook)

Copy the sentence from the material in which you last found the word used. Underline the word.

Column 6—My sentences

Form original sentences using the word in its various forms so that you approach total familiarity with it. Try to compose the sentences so that the context will define the word. These will be of great help to you in your reviews and will also be of value when you get to the paragraph technique, which will be described next.

C. PARAGRAPH TECHNIQUE

You begin your study of a word when you fill in the columns of your Vocabulary Chart. However, you can't stop there if your objective is to learn to *use the word.* That's why you must look upon your chart work as only preliminary. There is more to be done before you can be satisfied that you have made an addition to your "use" vocabulary.

Assuming that you have numbered your entries, you are ready to begin a study unit as soon as you have a group of 5 words. Once you have organized your vocabulary work along these lines, you can make your next contribution to the basic 15-Minute-a-Day Plan, which thus far has covered the elimination of roadblocks, the training in reading words in groups, and the improvement of your comprehension.

Take one word each day. On one side of an index card write the word; on the other, the common meaning, any clue (etymology—prefix, etc.), and the various forms. This should take about a half minute, during the evening, so that you are prepared for the next day's practice.

In the morning put the card into your pocket or purse when you leave for the day. Sometime before lunch, take the card out. Don't look at it closely until you are certain the side containing only the word is facing you. Then try to recall the meaning, clue, and forms. Spend no more than 15 seconds on this procedure. If you can't remember, turn the card over and read the summary. Your next step is to compose and write out a *sentence using the word* on a scrap of paper. Read the sentence aloud. Throw the paper away.

During the afternoon repeat the whole process. However, when you get to the sentence, use a different form of the word. Again, in the evening, check your card, and then write another sentence, this time using a third form of the word (if it has more than one or two forms). Don't omit the oral reading. You want to be able to handle the word in your writing *and* speech.

The next day continue with your second card of the week. Check it; write a sentence; read it aloud—on three separate occasions. With training you will be able to do the practice work for any period of the day in less than a minute. You are not trying to create sentence masterpieces. Your main purpose is to look at the word, recall its meaning, write it in context, and say it.

By Friday evening you should have completed your work with 5 cards. That makes you ready for the paragraph technique, to be developed on weekends.

On *each* of these days, spread out the 5 cards on a table or desk. For a minute or so just look at the words. Try to build up a relationship among them that will suggest a topic for a paragraph.

This won't come easy at first. You are attempting to pull an idea out of the air and then work with words that are relatively new to you. But again it's a matter of mental set. You are forcing your mind to think creatively. After you have done a few of the paragraphs, you will be surprised at the ease with which you will "see" any number of topics in a group of unrelated words. You will find the exercise a real challenge, interesting to do, and perfectly possible to complete within a reasonable amount of time. My students, and I am including the least skillful, manage to compose original and sensible paragraphs in less than 15 minutes, after they have had the experience for a few weeks! Here's an example of how it's done.

Your aim is to write a short, meaningful paragraph containing all 5 words you have studied during the week. Suppose we take a set from among the many words you met in this chapter and trace the writing operation:

supercilious   debonair   mediocre   cursory   credulous

Perhaps one of the sentences you composed during the week or entered in your Vocabulary Chart will suggest something to you. If not, try to think of a person, place, or thing that could be described by the words. Or it may suddenly occur to you that *supercilious* and *mediocre* are rather contradictory of each other. This train of thought may lead you to think of someone who has a higher opinion of himself than he merits. Now you have a concrete idea, so you write:

Wilson's *supercilious* smile and *debonair* manner fooled most people. In their *credulous* acceptance of the man, they were easily convinced that he had superior abilities. However, one who gave him more than a *cursory* look soon discovered that he was far from the genius he pretended to be. In fact, his talents were quite *mediocre* when put to the test.

Or perhaps you thought of a supersalesman:

A *credulous* public had long been his victims. Never allowing people more than a *cursory* inspection of his product, he wore them down with his *debonair* disregard for the facts. In the face of his *supercilious* smile, one dared not question him. This made it possible for him to sell *mediocre* products with the air of one offering jewels.

Or you might have been in a romantic mood:

Charlton approached her with the *debonair* charm of a Continental. His reward was a *supercilious* smile that seemed to say that he was not worth more than *cursory* attention. Her attitude tested his *credulity* to the limit. Charlton couldn't believe that anyone would dare treat him as if he were a *mediocrity* among men.

You will note that in the last paragraph different forms of some of the words were used. This was in accordance with our suggestion that you develop flexibility in your handling of words so that you can select any form called for by the construction of the sentence.

Are you beginning to get the idea of how to write these paragraphs? Give your mind free rein and it will usually come up with a topic suitable enough to include at least a few of the words. Then the problem of adding the remaining ones becomes relatively simple since you have an idea to attach them to; getting started is generally the hardest part of this exercise.

Let's try the paragraph technique with another set:

apprehensive   carnage   antipathy   introvert   gregarious

You see *introvert* and *gregarious* and again find contrasting meanings. *Carnage* suggests war or battle, and you should be about ready for your first idea:

> Only the *gregarious* personality accepts the crowded life of an army camp uncomplainingly. To the *introvert*, the lack of privacy is a severe shock, and he approaches his barracks existence with a natural *antipathy*. Moreover, the withdrawn person cannot help feeling *apprehensive* about the *carnage* of battle he will one day have to witness.

Occasionally you may enjoy trying to fit serious-sounding words into a light subject. This gives you practice in developing further versatility with your vocabulary. For instance, with our second group we might try something like this:

> The new puppy could hardly be called an *introvert*, judging from the awful *carnage* he left in his wake the first time the family went out for the evening. Shoes strewn all over the living-room floor, overturned lamps, and slipcovers wildly disarrayed attested to his *gregarious* nature. He had to play with someone—or something. Obviously he had greeted the prospect of being left alone with considerable

antipathy. There may also have been in his mind the thought that henceforth we would be so *apprehensive* about what he might be up to that we would think twice before making a hermit out of him again.

Sometimes, if you can't think of anything special, a very ordinary daily occurrence offers interesting possibilities. Here's what can be done with bargain day at your favorite department store:

An *introvert* would not have set foot into the store that day. It required a highly *gregarious* nature to plunge oneself into the mass of shrill-voiced humanity that stormed about the counters and left the aisles littered with the *carnage* of the struggle for bargains. Even if one did not have an *antipathy* for crowds and noise, he would certainly feel *apprehensive* about his safety once caught in the surging mob.

To vary the procedure, you may want to compose oral paragraphs. Get an idea and then *talk it out,* inserting the study words at reasonable intervals. This will help you build up your speaking vocabulary, which for most people, it has been pointed out, is the weakest of all. The most important thing is not the topic or how you develop it. It's your use of the words.

You must be very persistent in developing the paragraph technique. Unless you force yourself to think with your newly acquired words and build thoughts with them, you will not be their complete master. And if you aren't, you will not experience the delight of finding them creeping into your speaking and writing activities, nor will they mean quite as much to you when you find them in material you read.

III. Reviewing the Words

If you follow the vocabulary plan faithfully, you give every word you enter in your Vocabulary Chart the complete treatment.

- You don't make a serious study of a word until you have seen or heard it at least a half dozen times.

- You intensify your memory image of the word by card practice during the week.

- You *use the word* in several original paragraphs that you compose over the weekend.

You would think that such a program is enough to set a word in your mind permanently. Usually, it is. However, no matter how strong an effort you make to retain material, there is a normal percentage of forgetting that must take place. This will be particularly true with some of the words you study but somehow don't manage to use very often. To guard against the possibility of your losing touch with too large a number of recently studied words, it is necessary to establish a systematic review that will refresh your memory from time to time. There are several ways this can be done. Each involves something old and something new, always a good idea when you are going over familiar ground.

A. THE CARDS

Keep a file of all the cards you fill out when you do your weekly word study. By alphabetizing them you will destroy the original order in which you studied each group of 5 words. When you have accumulated about 50 cards, start with the first 5 and spend a few minutes glancing at the words and trying to recall the meanings, clues, and forms. Those you have forgotten should be removed from the file and set aside. Then when you have 5 of these doubtful ones, substitute them for a new group and go through the customary routine. However, the weekend work should be slightly different, as you shall see in the next item.

B. THE PARAGRAPHS

To give you an example of the kind of paragraphs you should write for restudied words, I shall select 5 words at random and pretend that you found it necessary to do a weekly card drill with them for the second time:

recurrent credence carnivorous ominous copious

The weekend comes along and you are ready for the paragraph. You proceed as usual, looking for a topic that will enable you to use the words. *Carnivorous* seems to be most prominent, and perhaps it makes you think of a jungle beast. Whether this idea or another occurs to you, as soon as you have an acceptable topic you begin to write. However, this time you do not include the words. Instead, you insert spaces and, next to them, synonyms, thus:

Although Clauson had consumed _____ (plentiful) quantities of his favorite brandy, it was difficult not to place _____ (belief) in his tale of the huge tiger that periodically raided the village. _____ (repeated) references to this legendary beast by others had convinced most of us that the _____ (meat-eating) monster was a real although rarely seen threat. Any doubts

I might have had about the stories were dismissed when an _____ (threatening) snarl thrust itself through the darkness surrounding the camp fire. This was no time to argue.

carnivorous   ominous
credence   copious
        recurrent

Make a collection of such paragraphs and use them from time to time as a third review. After you have gone through a second card drill on a set of words, let a few weeks elapse and then take one of the "spaces" paragraphs, match the words with the synonyms next to the spaces, and put the material away for another day.

A continuous rotating plan such as outlined above—with the chart, cards, and paragraphs—will keep your growing stock of words in active use. The procedure will soon become a habit with you:

Select a word!

Study it!

Use it!

Review it, if necessary!

CHAPTER IX

STEP FIVE:

Shift into High!

Numerous experiments have demonstrated that many people tend to operate at less than their full capacities. They settle into a certain groove and stay there because they have convinced themselves that they have reached their limits. However, every year we see evidence that a few people consistently refuse to accept standards that are supposed to be maximum. They go on to greater heights to prove that records are made to be broken, that levels of achievement can be raised. Athletes are constantly running or swimming faster than ever before; jumping higher or longer; hurling, throwing, or batting objects farther. Scientists periodically effect breakthroughs—from new cures for diseases to trips to the planets.

Many theories are advanced for the steady march forward despite the natural tendency to accept what is as permanent. No factor is more significant than the willingness of the inventive few to break psychological blocks. They snort at terms like "incurable, not humanly possible, beyond bodily endurance, will last forever." They believe something can be done—and they go out and do it!

There is a valuable suggestion here for you and your reading problems. You are dissatisfied, but perhaps you, too, have convinced yourself that you are doing the best you can. True, you now know how to eliminate roadblocks, stretch your span, improve comprehension, enrich your vocabulary. Yet you may still be unable to overcome the feeling that all the new techniques will not help in the long run. Past experiences have not offered much encouragement.

If this is so, you must break through your own psychological block. You must prove to yourself that you *can* read faster, break your present record of *words-per-minute,* and having done it once or twice, keep on breaking it. Only then will yesterday's record become today's normal rate.

Let's say that right now you read about 200–250 wpm. This has been your rate for years. You have never seriously tried to go faster on a consistent basis. You have told yourself that stepping up your pace will only lead to confusion. Or you have been satisfied to offer yourself what seems like a reasonable excuse. You wanted to increase your rate but you didn't exactly know how. Well, now you do. The one thing that can hold you back hereafter is your own failure to exert the extra effort required to break old habits and establish new ones. You must start doing the impossible every day and stop thinking about the difficulties. YOU MUST PUSH YOURSELF!

You may have already given yourself a sample of what you can do under pressure. In one of the diagnostic tests you took in Chapter III, you were asked to force yourself to read faster than you normally do. You were probably able to increase your rate at least a little bit simply by concentrating on speed. Our objective in this chapter is to show you how to set up the last phase of your daily program. You will spend a few minutes each practice session pushing yourself to read a trifle faster than you did the day before. Once you have established in your mind that you *can* do it, you will have gotten over the mental barrier. Doubling your present reading rate, at the very least, will then become an achievable goal within a relatively short period of time.

Lest you get the impression that I am suggesting that you train yourself to read under a constant strain, let's look into the problem a bit further. As was said, most people use only a fraction of their maximum abilities. Thus our purpose in asking you to push yourself is to get you to the point in your reading skill where you are working at 100 per cent of your capacity. During your early practice sessions it will be quite a challenge to you to keep hustling along beyond what was formerly a comfortable, easy pace. But in the long run you will not be trying to do more than you can. You will be encouraging your "reading muscles" to function at their best. Once they have become accustomed to full output, they will fall into a pattern of operation that will be just as comfortable for you as your present one now is. The strain will disappear. What will remain is a remarkably accelerated normal reading rate.

You understand, of course, that anything said about an increased rate applies only to materials that you should be able to read at a faster pace than you now do. A basic premise we have already established is worth repeating: *sheer speed in itself, without reasonable comprehension, is worthless!* We have stressed how important it is to develop a flexible rate, one which enables you to make all the decisions about how fast you want to read a particular piece. You can eventually train yourself to operate much like a car with standard shifting gears. Sometimes, in rough going, you will proceed in first gear; at other times, in second; and, when you are out for a pleasure drive, you will *shift into high!*

The student, scientist, engineer, or doctor who is reading highly technical material must place comprehension first.

185

He should read only as fast as he can while readily absorbing the ideas or data. If 200 words per minute seem just right, that should be it. There should be no pushing under these circumstances. But as your normal reading speed improves, you will be surprised later on, however, when you find yourself confronted with complicated reading matter, that even then you will make slight increases in the rate at which you read.

A second kind of material that you should read at whatever rate is consistent with complete understanding is a book, article, or report that presents controversial ideas or seriously examines a topic in a scholarly or analytical way. You won't want to hurry past the author's conclusions. Moreover, he may write in so concentrated a style that every sentence gives much food for thought. Take your time. Get his point. You can go faster than with technical material, but not at your maximum rate.

Now, what about the reading that you do for fun, for relaxation—those pleasure trips you take through the sports, fashions, entertainment, or general-news sections of a newspaper; the light-fiction or novelty articles of magazines; or the detective stories that are so popular? If you are like most of us, these are the materials that get your day-to-day interest. And it is here that you must begin to push yourself. Almost at once you can increase your rate in recreational reading by 20 per cent. Eventually you should be able to cruise along at 400 to 500 words per minute. With the skill and confidence you will gradually acquire, you should then go on to those novels, short stories, plays, and other literary products you have been promising yourself you will one day read. "If I only had the time!" you've said again and again. Well, if you can train yourself to cover twice as many words per minute as you once did, *you won't even need extra time* to read more.

In order to maintain a consistent program of practice in pushing yourself, you will need to set up a chart in your notebook:

Date	Name of article, book, etc.	*W/P/M-Normal	W/P/M-Pushing

*Words Per Minute

Before I outline how you are to make the entries and what your daily practice sessions should consist of, I want you to be able to estimate your reading rate at any time, regardless of the nature of the material. We will use the article below to illustrate how to do the necessary arithmetic. Get a watch so that you can time yourself. When the second hand is approaching the "12" on the face of the watch, begin reading. Proceed at your normal rate. Don't try to push. When you have finished the piece, jot down the total number of seconds it took you.

Jai Alai . . .

There are very few jai alai players in the world. You can understand why, when you witness this lethal game—

when you learn that in one month of play at one court 23 players were injured—some requiring major surgery.

There are thousands of fanatic followers of this flamboyant sport, which may have originated with the Aztecs six centuries ago—but which, in its modern form, is generally credited to origin in the Basque mountains where, the old pros claim, the best equipment is still made.

Like the flavor of Basque olives, jai alai is difficult to capture in words—it's a subtle blend of anything but subtle action sports. It's played in a stadium known as a *fronton,* which has a court about half the size of a football gridiron. It's a ball game—and the ball's as hard as a bullet. This goatskin-covered missile is hurled and retrieved with a reed basket, in a game that's a combination of lacrosse, tennis and handball. The ball travels so fast you can barely see it—and the players contort themselves into bizarre attitudes in lunges that bring them crashing down on the concrete floor, for an immediate recoil to return the jet-propelled rock. This is the fantastic game of jai alai.

Like tennis, it is played in singles or doubles competition, in a court or *concha;* like handball, it is played with a hard rubber ball or *pelota;* like lacrosse, the ball is propelled with a reinforced scoop-shaped racquet, or *cesta.*

Jai alai was introduced to the United States in 1904 at the St. Louis World's Fair. Since then it has been publicly played in New York, New Orleans, Chicago, Hartford, and Miami. It's in Florida, where betting is legal, that turnstiles hum today. Between the first of the year and April 10, the season is at the high peak of excitement.

*　　　*　　　*

Now for the arithmetic:

1. Return to the article and count the total number of words in the first three lines. Your total is 33.

2. Divide 33 by 3 (number of lines), and you get 11 (average number of words per line).

3. Now count the lines in the article. You get 32.

4. 32 (number of lines) multiplied by 11 (words per line) equals approximately 350 (total number of words in the article).

5. Let's say it took you 70 seconds to complete your reading. 350 divided by 70 would give you an average of 5 words read per second.

6. Finally, you multiply 5 by 60 (number of seconds in a minute) and you have a rate of 300 wpm.

Now that you know how to work out your reading rate, we can get back to the chart. The *date* entry is to help you determine how long it took you to make a significant advance. The *name* of the article or selection will gradually give you a profile of the kind of material you prefer to read. This knowledge may suggest to you that you ought to try something different as a change of pace and interest.

The entries in the last two columns will not be valid unless, when you set up your practice sessions in "pushing," you make certain that you use material of similar difficulty and appeal on each occasion. You want to create the same challenge for both your normal rate and your accelerated one. Use selections that contain from 500 to 1,000 words. Divide each into two equal parts. Then you can read the first half at your normal rate and the second half under the speed pressure—and you will know that you have maintained a uniform quality.

To illustrate the general technique, we will turn to two paragraphs from the opening chapter of *A Tale of Two Cities,* by Charles Dickens. There is, incidentally, a general point that can be made here and that should apply to all your reading of fiction. When you come across

189

descriptive passages designed to give you the background of the story or a certain atmosphere, there is no reason to drag along the lines. The color and setting will come through much more clearly if you read briskly than if you insist on studying every last detail. We will get back to this problem in a future chapter, when we discuss *skimming*.

Both paragraphs are of equal length. Read the first one at your normal rate. No pushing—no straining. Don't forget to time yourself! When you have finished, make the entries in your notebook: the date, the name of the book, and your rate in words per minute.

NORMAL RATE

France, less favored on the whole as to matters spiritual than her sister of the shield and trident, rolled with exceeding smoothness downhill, making paper money and spending it. She entertained herself, besides, with such humane achievements as sentencing a youth to have his hands cut off, his tongue torn out with pincers, and his body burned alive, because he had not kneeled down in the rain to do honor to a dirty procession of monks which passed within his view, at a distance of some fifty or sixty yards. It is likely enough that, rooted in the woods of France and Norway, there were growing trees, when that sufferer was put to death, already marked by the Woodman, Fate, to come down and be sawn into boards, to make a certain movable framework with a sack and a knife in it, terrible in history. It is likely enough that in the rough outhouses of some tillers of the heavy lands adjacent to Paris, there were sheltered from the weather that very day, rude carts, bespattered with rustic mire, snuffed about by pigs, and roosted in by poultry, which the Farmer, Death, had already set apart to be his tumbrils of the Revolution. But that Woodman and that Farmer, though they work unceasingly, work silently, and no one heard them as they went about with muffled tread: the rather, forasmuch as to entertain any suspicion that they were awake, was to be atheistical and traitorous.

You count the words in the first 3 lines and divide by 3 to get your average words per line. Multiply this result by the number of lines in the passage. Do it now, before you read the next sentence in this paragraph. Your result should be approximately 230 words in all. Finally, work out the words per second and then multiply by 60 to get the words per minute. Make the notebook entry.

Now we're ready for the pushing exercise. Forget about eliminating roadblocks or stretching your recognition span when you do the forced-speed drill. We don't want anything to interfere with your concentration on reading as fast as you can. Besides, if you do make the conscious effort to move right along, you won't have time for roadblocks and you will be indirectly giving yourself the finest possible training in increasing your recognition span. Get ready to time yourself. If it took you almost a minute to read the first paragraph, make up your mind to do this one in less than 50 seconds. There will be a brief comprehension test at the end to enable you to prove to yourself that you got the important ideas in both selections, even though you were straining for speed in the second.

REMEMBER:

You don't have to look at every word!
You don't have to study every detail!

All you want to know is what England was
like in those days!

SPEED!   SPEED!   SPEED!

PUSH YOURSELF!

In England, there was scarcely an amount of order
and protection to justify much national boasting.
Daring burglaries by armed men, and highway rob-
beries, took place in the capital itself every night;
families were publicly cautioned not to go out of town
without removing their furniture to upholsterers'
warehouses of security; the highwayman in the dark
was a City tradesman in the light, and, being recognized and challenged by his fellow-tradesman whom
he stopped in his character of 'the Captain,' gallantly
shot him through the head and rode away; the mail
was waylaid by seven robbers, and the guard shot
three dead, and then got shot dead himself by the
other four, 'in consequence of the failure of his am-
munition'; after which the mail was robbed in peace;
that magnificent potentate, the Lord Mayor of London, was made to stand and deliver on Turnham
Green, by one highwayman, who despoiled the illus-
trious creature in sight of all his retinue; prisoners in
London gaols fought battles with their turnkeys, and
the majesty of the law fired blunderbusses in among
them, loaded with rounds of shot and ball; thieves
snipped off diamond crosses from the necks of noble
lords at Court drawing-rooms; musketeers went into
St. Giles's, to search for contraband goods, and the
mob fired on the musketeers, and the musketeers
fired on the mob, and nobody thought any of these
occurrences much out of the common way.

*   *   *

Do your words-per-minute calculations now and make the entries in your notebook. If you really pushed all the way, there should have been a significant increase. And to check your comprehension, here is the test.

COMPREHENSION TEST

From the five statements below, select the two that most accurately cover the *main ideas* in each paragraph.

_____ 1. A man in France had his tongue cut out.

_____ 2. There was much lawlessness in England.

_____ 3. The Mayor of London was robbed.

_____ 4. Abuses in France were already sowing the seeds of rebellion.

_____ 5. Tradesmen were frequently thieves at night.

ANSWERS: The correct ones are *not* one, three, and five.

I shall now give you two more sets of exercises so that you can become thoroughly familiar with the techniques you are to use in setting up your daily practice sessions in pushing your reading rate. For a while, when you force yourself to read faster, you will continue to feel uncomfortable and will have doubts about your comprehension. If you are persistent, however, you will weather this trial period and will gradually become more and more confident. When *both* of the last two columns in your chart show steady increases, you will know that you are making real progress.

With each of the sets below:

1. Read the first part at your regular rate.
2. Work out your words-per-minute speed.
3. Make the notebook entries.
4. Read the second part at your pushing rate.

5. Again make your entries for words-per-minute.
6. Check your comprehension with the test that follows the second part in each set.

SET I

Slow, Slow—Quick, Quick
BY GEORGE DUKE

[Normal Speed]

"When we get to Florida, we don't want to make fools of ourselves . . . so we've hired a private dancing instructor!" This female proclamation unraveled to mean that our group would be a bunch of clods if we couldn't cha-cha-cha, fandango, tarantella and rock 'n' roll like seasoned Murrays. To remedy this fate, a Mr. Peter Patter would bring his practice records and powdered floor wax to one of our homes twice weekly until we left for our vacation, a slickly trained troupe of dancing fools.

The first lesson began with Mr. Patter observing, while we self-consciously dipped and circled about him. I was sure he was deciding he might as well pack up his sapphire needle and patent leather pumps and leave after seeing our polished 1939 junior prom style, when he said: "I can see it will be some time before we get to those cha-cha-chas you talked about. Tonight we'll concentrate on the basic box step." Someone courageously explained that we knew all about those simple basics, having all attended Miss Simpkin's Fortnightly Dancing School years ago . . . "so let's go on, unless we're too advanced for Mr. Patter?"

The third lesson—after we had learned that dancers should glide from the hips, lead with the upper body, do the box step in right angles—we were introduced to the rhumba. "Now we're getting somewhere," I said, with my usual gift for turning a brilliant and apt phrase.

194

Where I got, unfortunately, was on the basement stairs. This may not seem odd to you, until I tell why I was there. The rhumba, Mr. Patter explained, has a charming hip rhythm, accomplished by throwing one's hips opposite to the natural way they move when one places one's weight on one's legs. For example, rhumba hips go the way hips go when one walks up stairs.

The women caught on, and were jiggling around the floor with South American abandon in no time. One of the husbands (a salesman who takes a lot of out-of-town business trips) smugly whipped his derrière around with gelatinous authority. The rest of us burned—then all were relieved, except me.

"Mr. Duke," Mr. Patter said, as he undulated my way, "you just don't seem to be applying yourself. Here, try it with me." Clenching my teeth, I shifted my sacrum with determined vigor. "No, no, no, Mr. Duke . . . you're placing the weight on the wrong foot!" He didn't mean his, although at the moment I wished he did; he meant that my hips refused to behave abnormally, as required by his Cugat record. So—I was assigned the basement stairs, where I soon learned to rhumba with proper grace. In fact, Mr. Patter had the class gather around and admire my rhythmic motion, as I plunged up and down the steps.

Our last class was tonight. We've all packed our cars, so we can get an early start for Florida in the morning. Although we never got to the cha-cha-cha, we've mastered the rhumba. I'm looking forward to discovering an authentic Latin-American nightspot, where I can show off my rhumba motion—provided, of course, there is a stairway near the bongos, and I can find a partner who can follow my escalator style.

———

COMPREHENSION TEST

Select the two statements that most accurately cover the main ideas in each part.

_____ 1. According to Mr. Patter, the couples didn't dance correctly.

_____ 2. Some vacationing couples hired a very strict instructor to teach them the latest steps.

_____ 3. Mr. Patter wore patent leather pumps.

_____ 4. The author found he could dance best on the basement stairs.

_____ 5. Mr. Duke didn't make very much progress with his lessons.

ANSWERS: One, three, and four are *not* correct.

SET II

120—And Like It!

BY JACK MABLEY

[*Normal Speed*]

Anybody can have a good time out on the golf course when he shoots 75 or 80. It takes a golfer of character, a person with nerves of steel and the determination of a lion to shoot 120 and walk off the 18th green with a smile.

120—and like it? Well, we don't like the 120, but we do like golf. The trick is to be serious about the game— but not too serious. You never stop trying to better your score, but you don't live and die with every shot.

YOUR EQUIPMENT: Your game is only as good as your clubs. My equipment helps explain my score. It is Alex Gilchrist unmatched with Thistle putter—two woods, and irons number 2, 4, 6, and 8, or maybe it's 9. The number is worn off. Most of these clubs are survivors of a set I bought for $5.98 with bag and a box of sand for teeing up the ball. I shot a 47 for nine holes with these clubs, and if I could do it once I can do it again with the same tools. Or can I?

WATER HOLES: Always use ten-cent repainted balls at water holes. Only new and expensive balls go into the water. (A water hole is no place for character, nerves of steel, or the determination of a lion. Let's be practical about this thing.)

YOUR SLICE: There are two approaches to curing a slice. The Pros' way—push your right thumb around to the left side of your driver. For this lesson they charge you ten bucks. The Lousy Golf way—face the cows over in the field to your left, hit the ball at an angle 45 degrees to the left of the hole, and if your slice is properly trained it will come to rest right in line with the hole.

Left-handed golfers reverse everything. When you're facing south, and the ball curves west, do you call it a hook or a slice?

[Pushing Speed]

CADDY CARS: If you like swimming in your over-shoes you'll love these little electric carts that haul you around the golf course. They have some advantages over boy caddies—they don't snicker when you drive and they can't count your strokes when you're trying to pick up a little lost ground. They don't complain, either. But they eliminate the exercise, and if a 120-golfer isn't out there for the exercise I don't know what he IS seeking.

FRINGE BENEFITS: The Lousy Golfer has advantages in golfing that the expert never dreams of. In what other sport can you get the equivalent of a college education? The 120-golfer gets laboratory sessions in higher mathematics, nature study, physical culture, psychology, and debating.

CHEAT? Never. Obey every rule, every regulation, every local variation down to the last letter and comma and period. Avoid such dodges as "winter rules." Never concede a putt to yourself. Shoot from the meanest gopher hole even if you have to dig your way in with a 9-iron. Cheating—or shall we charitably call it a casual approach to the rules—is for the 70 and 80 shooters. Also we lose part of our alibi if we don't adhere strictly to the rule book.

THE FUTURE: Here is the most glorious part of Lousy Golf. What has the expert got to look forward to? Where is the 68 shooter going? 67? Ha. The low-handicap player shoots a 74 or 72 and he's had it, he's shot his wad. He has nothing to look forward to but memories.

If he shoots 90 or 100, he's ready for the knife. If WE shoot 100 it calls for a celebration.

The experts have nowhere to go but down. We can only go up. Aren't we the smart ones?

COMPREHENSION TEST

Select one out of each of the sets of three statements that refers to the main idea in each part.

Part I

_____ 1. Repainted balls should be used at water holes.

_____ 2. Left-handed golfers should reverse every-thing.

_____ 3. Inferior golfers can have fun even with poor equipment and skill.

Part II

_____ 1. A caddy car is very useful.

_____ 2. The poor golfer has the advantage of a good incentive always before him, so he can disdain mechanical equipment and cheating.

_____ 3. A poor golfer can get the equivalent of a college education.

ANSWERS: The correct choices are number two in the second part and number three in the first part.

Although we are coming to the end of this chapter, your "pushing" practice has only just begun. You now know how to force yourself to lift your reading rate to your maximum capacities. Success will not come in a matter of days or a few weeks. You are in the process of breaking a lifelong habit and you must be patient. But steady, dogged practice will bring noticeable results almost every day. And in a few months you won't have to push any more. You will have broken through your speed barrier.

So spend the suggested 3 minutes daily on a selection you take from a newspaper, magazine, or book. Divide the piece into approximately equal parts and proceed with your normal-rate and pushing-rate drills. In each instance, a good way to check your comprehension is to set up a test similar to the ones you have been taking. Preparing an examination is practically as good a review as taking one. And don't forget your notebook!

One final caution: don't expect to continue to increase your rate indefinitely. How far you will go depends upon your basic capacities. Experiments have shown that, with proper practice, almost everyone can make a 20 to 50 per cent improvement in reading speed. Howver, for some people this will mean a jump from 150–200 words per minute to 180–300 words per minute. And for them it will represent fine progress indeed. Others may eventually manage 500 words-per-minute without straining. A very small number will be able to report more than a thousand *wpm*.

You will know when you have reached your top level by the amount of rate increase continued practice brings. Your best indication will be the results of the last two columns in your daily speed chart. If over a period of weeks, the normal and pushing rates show little difference, you will be able to assume that you are approaching your full capacity. At this time you should take a vacation of a week or so from your speed training. Then resume your exercises. Watch the column results again. Check to see whether you haven't gone back to some old bad habit that you thought you had eliminated. If after all this there is still no progress, you can rest on your laurels. An occasional practice session will enable you to maintain your newly developed reading rate.

CHAPTER X

The Five-Step Plan: 15 Minutes a Day!

If you have come this far . . .

If you have not put the book aside with words like

Some day when I have more time . . .

If you have already made preliminary attempts to master the various techniques . . .

You can be sure of two things!

You have the patience and determination to finish what you have set out to do.

You will progress steadily, perhaps quite rapidly, toward your goal of improving your reading habits.

Chapters V through IX were the test. Had you lacked the ability to stick to a job after it was undertaken, you would have quit long ago. As you read through the previous five chapters, you had repeated evidence that only consistent effort will bring results. It is not unusual, when such a realization comes to a person, for an initial enthusiasm and willingness to work to disappear quickly. Unfortunately, too many of us seek a magic formula to accomplish something instead of relying upon a little self-discipline and lots of practice.

But you haven't given up. You're still willing to go on. Good. From now on the road is downhill. You've gotten over the major obstacle—proving you have the will power to see your problem through. And you are ready to be told how to organize your daily practice sessions so that you get the most out of them. Follow the various plans faithfully. You will observe your skills increasing day by day. You will become a confident, effective reader.

DAILY PLAN

15 MINUTES A DAY

Step 1: Knock Out the Roadblocks! [See Chapter V]

Time: 2 minutes

Procedures: a. Take one bad habit at a time.

              b. Spend at least 2 weeks on it, 10 sessions altogether (weekends reserved for vocabulary practice).

              c. Vary the daily practice devices as much as possible.

For instance, if you are working on the elimination of *vocalization,* select a passage and on the first day check the sounds in your throat by placing your fingers on your "voice box." Read for 2 minutes, making certain there is no vibration.

The next day try the technique of blowing air out of your mouth as you read silently. The third day, spend 2 minutes reading as you breathe forcefully through your mouth. Improvise. Mix up your attack, but keep one objective before you at a time.

202

Step 2: Stretch Your Span! [See Chapter VI]

Time: 3 minutes

Procedures: a. Divide your practice time into two parts.

               b. Spend about 1 minute each day on the card exercises described in Chapter VI.

               c. Do as many cards as you can *comfortably* in the time allotted and then put the material aside.

               d. After a few weeks, when you handle the phrase cards expertly, try some of the vertical-column exercises.

               e. Then vary your 1-minute phrase practice from one type of exercise to the other during the week.

               f. Spend two minutes daily on the rhythm exercises.

               g. Start each day's practice at this point by going through Rhythm Drill 1 to get into the proper groove.

               h. Then, for the remainder of the time, transfer this training to some of the other rhythm exercises described in Chapter VI.

               i. Keep doing this for a few weeks.

               j. After you are sure you are habitually reading in word groups, go on to selections that have been marked off in advance with a certain number of stops per line.

Use the material in Chapter VI as long as you can. When it no longer brings you the value of newness, construct some additional exercises of your own.

Don't try to rush things. If you have to start with 3-word phrase cards, do so; and don't increase them to 4- or

5-word groups until you are sure you are ready to stretch your span a little wider. Similarly, if you have to begin with four stops per line in the rhythm exercises or the marked off passages, be patient. The three- and two-stop exercises can wait until you have developed the necessary confidence to move through them with good comprehension. Steady progress is definitely preferable to frustration.

Step 3: Look for the Keys! [See Chapter VII]

Time: 5 minutes

Procedures: a. There is enough material in Chapter VII to last you for the first few weeks of comprehension training.

b. Take one exercise a day and spend your 5 minutes reading it and answering the questions.

c. You will find additional exercises in the Appendix. Use these, too.

d. When you run out of material in the book, prepare exercises yourself. As was pointed out before, the mere act of setting up questions on the contents of a selection gives training almost as valuable as answering someone else's test.

e. If you wish to get more ready-made practice passages, you can write to the various state education departments or municipal and Federal civil-service bureaus. Ask them to send you typical reading questions given on examinations conducted under their supervision. Usually the material is free, or there is only a nominal charge.

However, let me repeat. You will do very well if you look for the keys on your own. *Know-*

ing how to get what you should out of your reading is the main objective. Constant application of this skill must of itself bring improvement.

Step 4: Build Your Vocabulary! [See Chapter VIII]

Time: 2 minutes

Procedures: a. Follow the daily and weekend instructions outlined in Chapter VIII.

b. Make no effort to find new words to add to the ones entered in your vocabulary chart when you do the daily 15-minute drills. Your entire attention should be centered on developing the various skills involved, and you should not allow word-consciousness to interfere. Pick your words from the materials you read at other times.

c. As your original vocabulary paragraphs increase in number, you can use them for some of the practice exercises recommended in connection with the previous three steps.

Another important point must be repeated. The daily practice sessions can and should be completed in 15 minutes. However, you must apply your gradually improving skills to general reading as often as possible. Practice without performance will slow up your progress. Do not let a day go by without reading something besides your newspaper. Here, too, get variety. Try them all—books, magazines, pamphlets, etc.

Step 5: Shift into High! [See Chapter IX]

Time: 3 minutes

Procedures: a. Remember to choose a single selection that

205

you can divide into roughly equal parts, about 350–500 words each.

b. Spend the first minute reading the first half of the selection at your non-pushing rate.

c. Record the words-per-minute in your notebook chart.

d. Now read the second half at a forced speed. Time your "high gear" reading effort and enter the result in the last column of your chart.

e. The extra minute here is for the chart entries and the possibility that the passages may not be of exactly equal length.

The second reading may not always be much faster than the first. It may show only a slight increase in speed over the first. But significant results will be determined by comparing words-per-minute entries over a period of weeks, not days. Keep "pushing" and the numbers in both of the last two columns of your chart will steadily increase.

LONG-RANGE PLAN

Every few weeks, take stock. If you find that you have eliminated all your roadblocks, make some adjustments in your schedule. Spend only a few minutes a week on Step 1 to make sure you do not slip back. Use the extra time available on what seems to be your greatest difficulty.

You will reach the point where you find yourself making a specific number of stops per line almost effortlessly. Further experimentation may convince you that this is your best pace for the time being. You can cut down on your phrase practice until you feel that you have mastered the rhythm so well that you want to try to move on to the next pattern. Then you can resume the phrase practice, with a wider span in the exercises.

Let's say you eventually get to the three-stop-per-line stage and you feel quite comfortable with this rhythm. Transfer the phrase-practice time to the "pushing" drills. Soon thereafter you may want to attempt the two-stop-per-line pattern. Set up the appropriate drills and include phrase practice in your daily sessions once more.

Your over-all objective should be the elimination of most of the time devoted to the mechanical problems of reading (roadblocks and recognition span drills) in favor of concentration on rapid comprehension and vocabulary enrichment. And beyond this point will come the time when you need practically no direct daily drills at all. You will have establshed good habits and these will be strengthened automatically as you continue to expand your general reading activities.

As noted earlier, if you become bored with your daily practice sessions, take time off for a week or so. Get back to work as soon as you feel better motivated. Give yourself a big lift by convincing yourself that improving your reading ability will not take a lifetime. The job can be done in months. Best of all, the skills developed can be maintained by participation in one of life's most exciting forms of recreation—reading!

CHAPTER XI

Skim Reading

Skimming is a technique you developed a long time ago. From your earliest experiences as an independent reader, you seemed to be able to apply this skill in a perfectly natural way. The first time you voluntarily picked up a collection of stories, you didn't automatically turn to the opening page and begin reading. More likely, you browsed through the table of contents until a particular title struck your fancy. Then you turned to the story, glanced rapidly over the contents of a page or two, and decided quickly whether you had made a good choice.

You didn't have to be told by your teachers to follow this procedure. It was an extension of a habit formed at infancy. You learned early to taste a new food before committing yourself to eating it. As you grew older, you followed the same impulse. It became routine for you to try on several articles of clothing before selecting one to wear, to test ocean or lake water before plunging in, to "size up" a person before getting better acquainted. Thus, when your reading activities passed the early stages, it wasn't necessary to explain the idea of sampling to you. It had become a part of your normal human reaction to challenging situations.

When you began to use a dictionary, you had little difficulty training your eyes to drift down a page until you spotted the word you were after. You did the same thing to locate a topic in the index of a book, a number in a telephone directory, the scheduled arrival or departure time of a train in a timetable.

Since you have done considerable skim reading before, you may be wondering why additional training in this skill wasn't included in some of the previous chapters. A good reason can be found in what a dictionary says about *skimming:* "to pass over lightly or hastily; to glide or skip along the surface; especially, to give a cursory glance or consideration."

As you can see by its definition, skimming is not the kind of reading you have been told to do to achieve full comprehension. You can hardly get everything you should out of a selection if you pass over it lightly, skip about, or give it just a cursory glance.

The point is, of course, that when you are skimming your objectives are not the same as when you are interested in all the ideas, important details, and other features of a writer's material. Not only is the approach different, but certain adjustments must sometimes be made in the eye movements as well. So you can see that it would be very confusing to train yourself to adopt one set of procedures for regular reading and simultaneously practice another for skimming.

The last thing I want you to do is develop a helter-skelter pattern of reading. Too many people become poor readers precisely because they set up speed as their sole objective and race through material without knowing what to look for and without any real purpose. They skim-read not when the occasion warrants it but as if they knew no other way. They have never quite mastered the fundamentals, so they do not have an assortment of skills with which to meet a specific reading situation.

That's why this chapter has come at the very end. Its pages should be labeled somewhat like a Christmas gift bought in November: "Not to be opened until . . ."—in this case, until you have worked with the Five-Step Plan long enough to have shown marked improvement in your normal rate and comprehension, and your new reading habits have become firmly established.

Regard skimming as an extra, a fine point. Forget about it for at least a few months after you have started your reading-improvement program. And when you do get around to attempting to extend your skim-reading ability, remember that this is a special skill to be reserved for special occasions.

There are two broad areas in which skimming is useful and often essential. The techniques recommended for one differ to some extent from those of the other. We will examine each separately and show you how to improve the skills you already possess in this field. In the course of your training you will perhaps be able to join the group of readers who can achieve a rate of 1,000 words (or more) per minute when it suits their purpose.

I. Skimming for Specific Items of Information

Almost every day you find it necessary to check the spelling or meaning of a word; verify a name, address, or date; locate a particular fact; or glance again through something you have read before in order to refresh your memory about some detail. When this need arises, you turn to reference works—dictionaries, encyclopedias, almanacs, directories, guides of various descriptions—or to the previously read material.

In either case, you aren't interested in the entire book

at the moment of your research, or even the contents of any page you consult. What you are after is generally a very brief item of no more than a line or two. You recognize it as soon as you see it because you haven't approached the information with a complete blank in your mind. You already know all or part of the item if you are merely checking, or you have decided in advance what to look for and can rapidly eliminate every detail except the one you are seeking.

The material in the reference works you have consulted in the past is ordinarily arranged in columns. Your prior experience, therefore, should have made you fairly familiar with the technique of skimming down a relatively narrow column of print. You can easily train yourself to apply this skill to other materials as well.

Let's analyze what happens when your eyes begin to slide down a column of words, names, or figures. You *don't actually read* each entry. As a matter of fact, you don't even look for the particular bit of information you want. Whether you have realized this before or not, what you do is let your eyes drift past each item and wait for the one you are seeking to hit your consciousness. As your glance moves down a page, you are vaguely aware of other word or name images, but you react positively only when the right one comes along. You don't go after it; you let it come to you. To convince yourself that this is so, try the two exercises that follow.

Words

Start counting mentally from one to fifteen. Let your eyes move down the columns of words below, and before you have counted to the last number, see whether you can locate the word *industrious*.

idea
ignorant
illustrate
imitate
immediately
immigrant
increase
independence
independent
industrial
industrious
industry
influence

impatient
importance
important
impossible
improvement
include
information
injure
injury
innocence
inquire
insane

Words and numbers

Again count the same way. This time find the Smith who lives at 1239 Tinton Avenue. Your glance should focus on a point between the names and the addresses.

Smith, Helen	2100 University Avenue
Smith, Helen	4215 Wickham Avenue
Smith, Henry	692 Claremont Drive
Smith, Henry	1160 Fulton Place
Smith, Henry	1722 Dorset Road
Smith, Henry	2288 Wallace Avenue
Smith, Henry	1640 East 50 Street
Smith, Henry	1700 West 98 Street
Smith, Henry	1239 Grant Boulevard
Smith, Henry	1888 Phelan Street
Smith, Henry	159 Bailey Court
Smith, Henry	84 East 222 Street
Smith, Henry	225 West 99 Street
Smith, Henry	1239 Tinton Avenue
Smith, Henry	1653 Brookdale Street
Smith, Herbert	1892 Eastchester Avenue

Smith, Herbert	38 Brook Drive
Smith, Herbert	922 Clinton Road
Smith, Herbert	889 Arrow Avenue
Smith, Herbert	554 Clay Avenue
Smith, Herbert	1189 Southern Place
Smith, Herman	335 Undercliff Street
Smith, Herman	8 Suffolk Avenue
Smith, Hilda	45 Holland Place
Smith, Horace	667 West 59 Street

You were able to pick out the word and the name, I'm sure, despite the fact that your mind was busy counting up to fifteen. With such interference, you could not have done so had you been concentrating fully on each of the column entries. However, you were after a preset image and you needed only part of your attention to accomplish your objective.

This is the skill you have exercised so often before. With little additional training you can learn to apply it to any line of print, whether it is the width of a word, a phrase, a newspaper-type column, or the 10-to-12-word span in a book. Use exactly the technique that has just been demonstrated whenever you are skimming for information. Focus your eyes on an imaginary line drawn down the center of the column or page you are consulting. Let your glance drift steadily downward. Allow no more than one stop per line and make no lateral movements. Take full advantage of your peripheral vision so that you cover practically the full line of print. Wait until the image you will recognize hits your consciousness. And keep going rapidly until it does! Of course when you do reach the desired point, you read all that is necessary with your normal attention to detail—and then out you go. Skim the material that is of no immediate interest to you, not the information you are seeking.

Each of the practice exercises that follow contains two

training suggestions. The time limit will help you gauge the speed at which you should skim. The advance question will indicate a typical bit of information you might be looking for if you were consulting a reference work or were checking a passage you had read before in order to remind yourself of a fact.

Skimming for Specific Items of Information—Exercise 1

Maximum time: 15 seconds

Question: What is the best old-model car for a beginner to choose for remodeling?

Reminders

Focus down the center of the column.

Slide right past material that does not contribute to answering your question.

Wait for key words to guide you to the item of information you are seeking. In this selection *old-model* connected with *beginner* will be the signal to your mind to stop skimming and start full concentration.

Crank Her Up Again

The fifty-year-old car seen in parades and exhibits may have been kept on blocks in someone's garage. More likely the car has been reassembled with loving care by one of the many persons who now have the old car restoration fever.

A car is an antique at 25, but enthusiasts seek even earlier models down to the horseless carriage days. These old cars are usually found in broken-down condition, at a cost of a few dollars to several hundred, depending on age, rarity, and condition. The market for old cars is expanding as the hobby grows, and the going price of, say a 1914 Stutz Bearcat, is clearly fixed. The Mercer Raceabout is today the most sought after and valued of antique automobiles. Other names to bring back the early beginnings of a wonderful industry are the American roadster, the giant Simplex, the Winton Six, the Franklin limousine or a Chadwick, the first supercharged car.

A beginner will probably choose a Model T Ford; it is easy to work on—even for an amateur, and parts are easily secured. Many hours of search, labor and mechanical work must go into bringing the car back to driving order and appearance. The first job is to find out how that particular model looked and operated—in every detail, for to have value, authenticity and interest, the old-timer must not be modernized or altered from its original state, construction, or mechanical workings.

If you were able (within the 15-second limit) to identify the Model T Ford as the best for a beginner to choose, you were skimming along at a rate of more than 800 words per minute!

Skimming for Specific Items of Information—Exercise 2

Maximum time: 20 seconds

Question: At what time of the year does the cutting of Christmas trees take place?

Down the center of the column!

No more than one step per line!

The word *cutting* is the clue to the answer to your question. Let it be your guide.

This time pretend that you have decided to get your own Christmas tree. You are not interested in the details of the tree business. All you want to know is when to cut so that you don't ruin the tree.

The Story of 30,000,000 Christmas Trees

Have you ever felt a twinge when you looked at beautifully decorated Christmas trees? That it was a shame to cut them down? Don't feel sad. The trees that delight young and old are usually doomed trees that would have died from root or sunlight starvation if they had not been cut. The thinning of the forests actually improves them, and in any event, none of the many large companies that harvest Christmas trees—it's an annual retail $77,000,000 industry—could afford bad forest practice.

Among the largest Christmas tree sources are logging companies with acres of reforestation projects. Seedlings pop up by thousands around parent seed trees. As the young trees grow, overcrowding becomes fatal. So Christmas tree cutters are called in to thin the land.

Many other Christmas tree farms are found on land logged off. There Christmas tree farmers thin out the seedlings before they have a chance to spoil each other's shape, and prune off lower limbs to make slower rising, thickly limbed trees almost round (better-looking Christmas trees than those of yore).

By saving seed trees and careful thinning, owners keep a crop of trees coming in the most popular market size of five to seven feet. Oddly enough, the two things that would put a farm out of business are a few years of *no* cutting or a couple of seasons of exceptionally good conditions for tree growth. A tree growing faster than a foot a year would be too spindly for a Christmas tree.

The cutting operation begins after the first freeze. If trees are cut earlier, the sap is still up and needles quickly fall off. Trucked to special yards in heavily shaded timber where it is wet underfoot and cool all day, the trees are sorted for size and quality, trimmed and finally tied in bundles for shipping.

Only a very small percentage of these 30,000,000 trees is not sold. So never think a Christmas tree grower is wasteful—for his whole livelihood depends on good forest management.

To find out (in 20 seconds) that the cutting operation begins after the first freeze required a skimming rate of more than 900 words per minute!

Skimming for Specific Items of Information—Exercise 3

Maximum time: 15 seconds

Question: What is the name of the catalysts that help us digest our food?

Reminders

Down the middle!
No more than one stop per line!
Note that these are full-size lines.

Excerpt from The Science Book of Wonder Drugs
BY DONALD G. COOLEY

How are you able to digest roast beef with such ridiculous ease?

Imagine the difficulties of a chemist who attempts to imitate this prodigious feat. He could treat the beef with powerful acids, distill it in a vacuum, whirl it in a centrifuge, apply terrific temperatures. After many days, he might be able to show you a few substances comparable to some products of digestion.

But you digest your food quickly and easily and with no little pleasure. You do so because you have body cells that produce exceedingly minute amounts of substances that act as catalysts. They make possible the combining of molecules into new substances by inducing chemical reactions that could not take place without the catalyst. All the processes of life—digestion, growth, muscle contraction, reproduction, nerve conduction, to mention a few—proceed only because catalysts see to it that the right chemicals are present at the right time. In a way a catalyst grasps molecules that will have nothing to do with each other, bangs them together so effectively that they combine to form different molecules, and performs thousands of these forced marriages (or, contrariwise, divorces molecular partners) in a fraction of a second.

Catalysts that work these miracles for you are known

218

as enzymes. Literally, enzyme means "in yeast." Something in yeast causes cereals and grapes to ferment, a very ancient discovery, and a far cry from present knowledge that the myriads of chemical reactions we call life take place only because enzymes make them possible.

*   *   *

Your rate, if you found the answer within the time limit, was about 1,000 words per minute.

Skimming for Specific Items of Information—Exercise 4

Maximum time: 10 seconds

Question: What is the oldest recorded date of the sport of falconry in England?

Reminders

Down the middle!
This is the fastest speed you have yet tried. If you succeed you will be skimming at a rate of about 1,200 words per minute!

The King's Hunter

A sound like a sudden rip of canvas. A flash of black plummeting across the blue sky faster than the pull of gravity. An explosive splintering of feathers. A falconer crosses the plain to the brush where his peregrine falcon has nailed a pheasant. He slips a hood over the falcon's head, takes her on his heavily gauntleted fist and puts the pheasant in his game bag.

This is the twentieth century. But the drama is identical to one practiced 5,000 years before. It is falconry, a hunting sport as old as recorded history. In antique China,

Japan, Arabia, Iran and Syria, artifacts depict falconry. On a bas-relief found in the ruins of Khorsabad there is a falconer bearing a hawk on his wrist. The oldest records of falconry in Europe are in the writings of Aristotle, Pliny and Martial. In England, from 860 to the middle of the seventeenth century, falconry was followed with an ardor no other sport had yet evoked. Louis XIV spent nearly every day of his reign afield at falconry. Today, it is still practiced ardently in Asia, not infrequently in European hunting preserves and sporadically in North America —where there are probably fewer than 100 practitioners.

* * *

The exercises you have just completed should have given you the idea of how to skim for items of information. Remember, you are not developing a new skill. You are applying an old one to new reading situations. Continue to perfect the technique involved by setting up advance questions about items of information and then finding the answers in various reference works. You already know how to figure out your words-per-minute rate. Do not forget, however, that skimming is an extra and should never become a substitute for your regular reading habits.

II. Skimming for Highlights

In the second area where you can use skimming to good advantage, your purpose is different. Now you want to get a bird's-eye view of a letter, article, story, editorial, or book. You are interested in a general impression, a main point or theme, the broad outlines of a plot, or perhaps just in finding out whether you should read the material more carefully a second time. Your objective is to pick out the highlights and to do so as quickly as possible.

Why is speed so important here? The most significant

reason is that reading situations that lend themselves readily to skimming for highlights usually find the reader short of time, or desirous of getting to something else quickly, or simply not wishing to waste time on material that he has no need to examine intensively. We might consider a few typical circumstances under which these conditions are present.

Every morning a pile of correspondence must be gone over in the average office. Business or professional time is too valuable to squander on trivial pieces of mail. That's why it is so useful to be able to skim through the batch of letters, set aside the ones that can be thrown out or answered at a later date, and select those that require a careful rereading.

Here's another instance. If you are like most busy people, you have only a short time to devote to your morning newspaper. Some people solve this problem by reading a few headlines, riffling through the sports or fashion pages, and winding up with the comics. But if you wish to be an informed citizen, you can use skimming to give you the highlights of the day's news and still have time left for your favorite features.

If you are a student or technician you have to do extensive research occasionally with the aid of several books and periodicals. Rarely is there enough time to do this job in a leisurely fashion. Besides, one book may repeat in part the material found in another. There is no point in going over the same ground twice. Skimming can help you go through a dozen volumes, when necessary, in rapid style while you concentrate on only the sections that are pertinent to your research problem.

And what about the recreational reading you are supposed to get into the habit of doing on a regular basis?

You will probably have to snatch an hour or so from a full day. This means that you won't be able to finish the book you choose in one sitting. Each time you get back to it you will experience difficulty in picking up the thread of the narrative or ideas unless you employ your skimming ability. If you learn to glance rapidly through the highlights of a few pages before the point at which you stopped reading, you will quickly be able to continue, with little loss of time or sequence.

Skimming is also very helpful in the selection of a book to read. In no time at all you can leaf through a few chapters, get a quick preview, and decide whether this is your kind of reading material. You can thus avoid the frustration of plodding along for fifty or a hundred pages and then giving up in disgust. The same procedure, incidentally, can be used when you have to study a part of a book. A rapid look at the text to be mastered gives you an over-all view of the subject matter and helps you decide what pages will need your closest attention.

From the foregoing examples you can understand why I said that the purpose in skimming for highlights is different from that of looking for a specific item of information. Your center of attention is on the whole of a selection, not on a small detail in it. The difference extends also to the eye movements.

When your glance is moving down a page in search of a particular bit of information, you can't permit any skipping of lines. If you do you may go right past the item you want to find. In skimming for highlights, you do not plan in advance to pick out certain facts or details. Your main concern is to get the general notion of the contents quickly. Therefore, you can skip here and there, since your failure to absorb a few details more or less in a long description, for example, will not materially affect your understanding of the story. Obviously this makes it inadvisable to focus steadily on a set point in a line. Your eyes must be free to wander about on the page.

That's why it is impossible to suggest a pattern of eye movements for highlight skimming. However, certain procedures can be recommended. You can use them separately or in combination, depending upon the material you are skimming. Each will be illustrated in the exercises that follow.

Skimming for Highlights—Exercise 1

Procedures: To prove that you can skip about as you move down a paragraph, we will try an experiment. In the first selection below, you will find only key words printed, with the rest of the material omitted. Then, you will take a comprehension test. Finally, you will be able to read the original article to check your results.

Maximum time: 10 seconds

——————— blue-green depths ————————
————————————— a strange battle ———————
————————————— a two-foot fish ———
the other a small crab ——————————————
————————————— delicate claws weak ———
————————————— not even move rapidly ———
Yet, within seconds ——————————————
————————————— the sharp-toothed fish ———
————————————— was fleeing wildly ———
Indian Ocean crab ——————————————
————————————— *had picked up a weapon* ———
————————————— a sea anemone ———
looks like a flower ——————————————

$\rule{2cm}{0.4pt}$ with powerful stingers $\rule{2cm}{0.4pt}$
$\rule{3cm}{0.4pt}$ In each of his claws
the crab had seized $\rule{3cm}{0.4pt}$
$\rule{2cm}{0.4pt}$ natural hand grenades $\rule{2cm}{0.4pt}$
$\rule{2cm}{0.4pt}$ and had hurled them $\rule{1cm}{0.4pt}$

COMPREHENSION TEST

1. It was a battle between
   a. a large crab and a small fish
   b. a small crab and a large fish

2. The winner was
   a. the crab
   b. the fish

3. Victory was achieved by
   a. a vicious bite
   b. a hurled weapon

Original Article

The Incredible Crab

BY REED MILLARD

In the blue-green depths of the Indian Ocean, a strange battle seemed certain to come to a swift, deadly end. For one of the opponents was a two-foot fish with razor-sharp teeth, the other a small crab. The helpless crab's shell was not very hard, its delicate claws weak. It could not even move rapidly enough to escape. Yet, within seconds, the sharp-toothed fish was fleeing wildly. For this little Indian Ocean crab had done something incredible—something almost unheard of in nature. *He had picked up a weapon and used it against his adversary.* This crab's weapon was a sea anemone, a curious marine animal which looks like a flower and is equipped with powerful stingers capable of shocking and partially paralyzing many animals or fish they touch. In each of his claws, which are not affected by

224

the plant's sting, the crab had seized one of these natural hand grenades and had hurled them at his foe.

In the "highlight" version, you read slightly more than one third of the original article, yet you were able to answer all the comprehension questions correctly, I'm sure, while covering material at the rate of approximately 1,000 wpm!

Our experiment should prove to you that you can learn to skip—when you wish to do so!—without missing too much. Use your knowledge of how a paragraph is constructed. The first sentence may give you the main point, and you can slide right past the rest of it. If an article is full of statistics that merely point up the generalizations, you can ignore many of them. You won't remember them anyway unless you study them, and this is not your purpose in skimming. You need look at just enough to make the ideas clear.

Skimming for Highlights—Exercise 2

Procedures: This time, instead of omitting words, we will print the key phrases in **bold-face.** Try to focus only on the "highlights," and check your results with the comprehension test that follows.

Maximum time: 20 seconds

Traveling with a Camera
BY JOHN RYAN

There's no question that a **photographic record** of a **trip** helps to **prolong pleasure** in the **places** visited and the

225

people met, and also helps you share this pleasure with the people back home.

Professional photographers and serious amateurs take their cameras wherever they go. But some not-too-experienced travelers seem to feel self-conscious about doing so because a camera hanging around the neck or over a shoulder has become the badge of the tourist.

What's so wrong about being a tourist? The more I travel, the more I am pleased to be identified as an American tourist. Natives of foreign parts who look down their noses at tourists are not in the majority—and those that do are merely the ones who are jealous because they aren't touring in some foreign (to them) spot.

Getting back to the strap, slinging it over a shoulder is often inconvenient because it keeps slipping off. I've found it better to let the strap out to its fullest length and sling it across my chest—like the shoulder strap of a Sam Brown belt—pushing the camera around back of my hip when I'm walking through crowded streets; this leaves both hands free and prevents damage to the camera that might result from its banging into people or posts.

Most amateurs know enough to keep the strap around the neck when making pictures. (It's pretty horrifying to watch such an expensive piece of equipment get smaller and smaller as it sinks through the crystal clear waters of a tropical bay.) But in foreign restaurants you see many Americans who don't seem to realize that cameras are almost as negotiable as currency in some countries, and so are a great temptation to thieves.

When I go into a restaurant, or into a grill car on a train, I never put my camera even on a chair beside me. I put it at my feet and hook the strap around an ankle so that if I should try to leave without it I'd go flat on my face. And I never trust my camera to porters, baggage handlers, check room attendants, or hotel servants. When I have to leave it in a room or in a ship's cabin, I lock it in a suit-case.

COMPREHENSION TEST

Insert *T* or *F* in the spaces.

_____ You should avoid carrying a camera because it labels you a tourist.

_____ It is best to sling the camera strap across the chest, not over a shoulder.

_____ One must be careful about a camera in foreign restaurants.

_____ On a train, one should place his camera on the seat beside him.

ANSWERS: F, T, T, F.

Skimming for Highlights—Exercise 3

Procedures: Many articles, such as this one, make their point early and then repeat it several times. The major interest lies in the names and anecdotes that are used to introduce the human-interest angle. You can knife through the introductory material and go directly to the names and stories. In skimming here you can read the first paragraph rapidly, skip right down to *Jackie Cooper*, go through the three brief stories, and finish the 500 words in about 30 seconds. Bear in mind also that you will often come across a selection that discusses a subject about which you are quite well informed. Your attention logically belongs only on those paragraphs that present something unusual.

Academy Awards

The street of dreams come true is the long, carpeted aisle, when the world's finest motion picture talents and technicians walk to the dais to receive the awards of merit from the Academy of Motion Picture Arts and Sciences. For each selected winner there's Oscar—a gold-plated bronze statuette that has powerful influence in the celluloid world.

On a night in March, about 150 nominees will tensely wait while the master of ceremonies carefully tears open the sealed balloting returns secretly tabulated by the accounting firm of Price-Waterhouse. They'll quickly run over their prepared acceptance speeches, hope their television make-up is perfect—then, when the announcement is made, they'll probably forget the speeches and smear the make-up with tears of joy or disappointment.

After more than half a century, the Academy Awards ceremony is still the most emotion-charged spectacle in glamorous filmland. In all the world there is no greater assemblage of beauty and talent, eager and curious, than that greeting the yearly appearance of Oscar.

From the Academy's inception in 1927, all the entertainment-conscious world has awaited the Awards with interest. Radio and television now carry the emotion-charged event to hundreds of millions of movie fans all over the democratic world. Besides the thrill and surprise of learning who the best performers are at the same time they do, each ceremony has its unplanned vignettes of human interest that make it memorable.

At the fourth year banquet, Jackie Cooper competed with Lionel Barrymore for the top male honor. There was much speculation as to how the little boy would "take it" if he lost to the veteran actor. When the time came for Barrymore to claim his statuette, tired little "Skippy" was sound asleep on the lap of Marie Dressler—herself a winner that year.

Frank Capra presided as emcee in 1939. He proceeded with caution, certainly remembering the evening four years previously when he had been nominated. Will Rogers was moved to laudatory speech-making before announcing the winner, ending his speech with, "Frank, come and get it!" Frank Capra proceeded about forty feet before he realized that Will Rogers was motioning to Frank Lloyd, who won for "Mutiny on the Bounty." Capra calls his return to the table "the longest crawl on record."

When Gary Cooper won for his portrayal of "Sergeant York," he said: "I've been in the business sixteen years and sometimes dreamed I might get one of these things. That's all I can say . . . Funny, when I was dreaming, I always made a good speech."

It's the realization and the frustration of those dreams by the movie greats that charge each Awards ceremony with suspense and emotion. It's what makes the Academy Awards a thrilling spectacle for millions of Americans.

TEST ON HIGHLIGHTS:

Mark each statement with a T or F.

_____ Oscar is the first name of a great actor.

_____ The Awards are given world-wide coverage.

_____ Jackie Cooper fell asleep at one of the affairs.

_____ Frank Capra received an award from Will Rogers.

_____ Gary Cooper found he had little to say after all.

ANSWERS: F, T, T, F, T.

*   *   *

The major techniques for highlight skimming have been illustrated in the preceding exercises. It would be impractical, of course, to give you direct examples of procedures to be followed with entire books or batches of letters. However, one or more of the recommended devices can be applied successfully to any material. So that you can have available guides to proper skimming techniques, suppose we set down the most useful ones.

1. If the article, story, or book is written with proper attention to paragraph construction, you can get most of its ideas by reading the first sentence, perhaps one in the middle, and the last one of very long paragraphs.

2. When you come to extended scenic descriptions and you have no immediate interest in the beauty of the language, look at *only a sentence or two per page,* and then get on with the story.

3. In skimming through letters, first see who sent it. That may be enough in itself. If not, glance at the opening sentence, and if that doesn't make up your mind, read the last one. By that time you should know whether the letter is of any importance to you.

4. Don't waste time plowing through line after line of statistics that are offered in bunches to make the point. Leave the figures to readers who have serious use for them. Once you understand what the author is trying to prove, you can slide past the numbers.

5. If you wish to skim through serious material—an

editorial, for example—you can do this very successfully by simply stopping at only the phrases containing the longer words and occasionally glancing at a name or date. This requires a zigzag pattern of eye movements, but you will have little trouble in perfecting this technique after a few tries.

6. When you start a book, make a conscious effort to become familiar with the author's style. If he likes to stretch out his descriptions or analyses, uses dialogue to clinch a point he has already made, has a tendency to repeat, you can find valuable clues that will help you skip generously without loss of understanding.

7. In textbooks, use the illustrations, chapter headings, table of contents, and your knowledge of paragraph structure to give you a preview of the material you will study later. It is often a good idea, if the book is yours, to underline important statements as you study. Later on, when you review, you can skim through the subject matter, concentrating almost exclusively on the underlined portions. The latter will be enough to refresh your memory.

8. Newspaper editors know that their readers are often pressed for time. For this reason, a standard journalistic device is to give an outline of the main points of an article in the first sentence or two. Thus it is possible to skim a news item of more than 1,000 words in less than a minute by reading the first paragraph carefully and then reading only the first line of each paragraph thereafter. Unquestionably, you will not get as much out of the article as you would if you read every word, but if it is highlights you are after and you wish to skim, you will come away with a surprisingly good understanding of the contents. Try this with any newspaper piece. Read it skimmingly first, then closely. You will note that the main points have reached you either way.

*   *   *

Before this chapter comes to a close, let me caution you once more about skimming. It is an extra. It should be used only when it suits a special purpose. It is never as good as rapid reading for full comprehension.

Regard this technique as a two-edged sword. It can help you cut through material easily, but used unwisely it can cause serious injury to your normal reading habits.

Your primary objectives in your improvement program are

The fastest possible rate adjusted to purpose and material!
Full comprehension!

And ultimately

An open road to pleasure, recreation, mental enrichment—through the things you read!

APPENDIX

Appendix

How to Answer Reading Questions on Examinations

It has become standard practice to include reading comprehension questions in high school equivalency, civil service, College Board, achievement, and all sorts of professional qualifying examinations. Many candidates, despite good reading ability, fail to do justice to themselves because they haven't learned the special techniques required to handle such questions.

You have already had the opportunity of working with typical selections that tested your ability to interpret the printed word, especially in terms of the *Guide Questions* outlined in Chapter VII. Excerpts used by examiners come from a variety of sources: usually, nonfiction prose; less frequently, fiction; and least often, drama and poetry. The majority of the questions based on the test selections focus on main ideas, contributing details, and implied meanings. In recent years, somewhat more emphasis has been placed on other features like the writer's purpose, point of view, reliability, or style. Whatever the form of the excerpt or questions, the candidate is required to pick the correct answer from a number of possibilities, usually five.

The worst way for you to answer any question is to fish about among the choices until a likely-looking one gains your favor. Such an approach becomes confusing since, after a while, all the possibilities look sensible or every one looks unacceptable!

The proper way to answer comprehension questions on examinations is to use the *process of elimination*. You check each alternative against a set of standards and either cross it out for good reason or retain it until you have made your final choice. If you can eliminate four out of five possibilities, the remaining one must be the right one. Let's trace the steps you should follow.

A. The Test Selection

It may be a single paragraph of 100–150 words or several totaling 200 words or more. Occasionally, excerpts are only one or two sentences. Of course, the longer a selection is, or the more complicated, the more questions can be asked about it. At any rate, read the test passage carefully, but not so slowly that you get lost in detail and miss the main point. If necessary, go over it a second time, particularly if you cannot arrive at a satisfactory *key word* (see below). Although you are not being tested on the speed of your reading rate, you must realize that too much time spent on any one set of questions will reduce the time you have left to answer the remaining parts of the examination.

In some state tests, a "Listening Passage" has been introduced. A teacher reads the passage once. The candidates are then allowed to look at the questions and select the answers as the passage is read a second time. Obviously, the reaction to the questions during a listening exercise must be considerably faster than it need be when the test material can be looked at as often as necessary. You would do well, however, despite the time handicap, to train yourself to handle the "crossing out" phase of the elimination process mentally so that your answer choices are properly made.

B. The Elimination Process

1. MAIN IDEAS

The form of the questions varies here, although the purpose remains constant. You may be asked to choose the "best title," or the "phrase that best expresses the main idea," or the "phrase that best expresses the content of the passage," etc. After you have read the excerpt, you turn to the possible choices among the answers. Your objective is to eliminate the unacceptable ones. You do this by applying one or more of the following standards.

a. Key word

If you have understood the main idea, you should be able to answer this question: *What is the selection talking about?* Very often you will be aided in arriving at your answer by the number of times a particular word is repeated in the paragraph, either directly or by use of a synonym. You should be able to express the answer to the question in a word, if possible; two, at most. *The title you choose must contain these words (or synonyms for them)!* Otherwise you have made an improper choice. Therefore, you cross out all possibilities that do not contain the key words. Do it this way ruthlessly. Do not be misled by an interesting-sounding title that on closer inspection has no specific connection with the main idea expressed by the paragraph.

b. Only part

Your key-word method may eliminate some choices but still leave two or three possibilities. You now examine the remaining ones in turn. If one of them refers to something mentioned briefly in the paragraph but not continued, cross it out. The title must cover the contents of the selection as a whole, and you cannot accept any possibility that refers to only part of it.

c. Not mentioned

A suggested title may sound as if it might do because it is logical and related to the subject matter. But if the author did not talk about it, cross it out.

d. Read into

You must bear in mind that the purpose of the reading question is to determine whether you can interpret *what the writer said,* not what you believe he should have said or what he might have said had he known as much as you do about the subject. Don't allow yourself or the examiner to put words into the writer's mouth. Don't allow your opinions or private information to interfere with your comprehension. Cross out any possibility that "reads into" the paragraph ideas or conclusions that exist only in the mind of the reader or the questioner. Such titles are often given as bait to the unwary.

e. Contradictory

If as much as a single word of a possible title suggests a conclusion that is the opposite of what was intended by the author, cross it out. Anything partially contradictory is as unacceptable as if entirely so.

Now we will apply these five elimination techniques to a typical paragraph.

Test Paragraph Interpretation—Example I

THE PARAGRAPH

Shipping out food to the United States troops in all parts of the globe and supplying many foods for Great Britain during World War II brought about dehydration. Why carry tons of water? A fresh egg is three-quarters water, many meats contain more than two-thirds water, fresh vegetables and fruits about 90 per cent. Drying foods dates back many years, but this new process makes them a lot drier and the foods keep most of their original food value and flavor. Because of dehydration these foods do not need refrigeration, nor is it necessary to package them in tin and so they require much less space in packing. Putting dehydrated foods in water is like bringing them back to life. Many foods are edible in their dehydrated state, and thus can easily be included in emergency kits for troops.

1. THE MAIN IDEA QUESTION

The title below that best expresses the ideas of this paragraph is

1. Advantages of dehydrated foods
2. Water content of food
3. Dehydrated diets
4. Saving space in supply ships
5. How foods are dehydrated

Elimination Process

Your answer to the question, *What is this paragraph talking about?* should be *dehydrated foods*. These are your key words, and you proceed to cross out every possibility that does not contain them. Therefore, you eliminate

    2—because it contains only one of the key words (*food,* but not *dehydrated*)

    3—for the same reason (*dehydrated,* but not *food*)

    4—because it contains neither key word

This still leaves the choice between 1 and 5.

You examine 1 in terms of the additional standards:
Is it only part of the main idea?
    No. The entire paragraph talks about this point.
Is it mentioned?
    Definitely!
Is it "read into"?
    No. It is the author's conclusion.
Is it contradictory?
    No.
Therefore, 1 remains a possibility.

Now you turn to 5.
Is it only part of the main idea?
    If you examine the paragraph closely, you discover that nowhere is 5 actually discussed.

You need not bother with any further questions. You can cross out 5 at once. This leaves you with 1 as your final choice, the correct suggested title.

You can see the advantage of the process of elimination. You are forced to think with the author, arrive at *his* conclusion, and cross out possibilities because you have definite reasons for doing so. There is no wild guessing possible.

It may be that the method at first glance seems to be time-consuming. Remember that you are not yet familiar with the guide questions. Continued practice will enable you to use them more rapidly and to arrive at your reason for elimination without the need for applying all of them each time you examine the possibilities. With added experience, the right questions to ask will occur to you automatically.

2. DETAIL QUESTIONS

Here, too, you use the guide questions to leave you with the correct answer.

a. Key sentences

Detail questions require that you examine only part of the paragraph to prove that you can find the details that support the main idea. Therefore, you shift your concentration to individual sentences. Your first step is to locate the sentences in which the detail asked by the question is mentioned. Then you check the possibilities with your guides against what the sentence covers.

b. Not mentioned

Again, if a possibility is not mentioned in any sentence, out it goes.

c. Read into

If a possibility suggests something that was not in the author's mind, it is eliminated, too.

d. Contradictory

Any thought opposite to the one expressed in a key sentence also cannot be accepted.

Let's try the standards with the detail question asked on the paragraph just quoted above.

Dehydration is a method of

1. preparing food for troops
2. drying food to preserve it
3. packaging foodstuffs
4. keeping food dry
5. making food palatable

Keeping the guide questions in mind, you examine each possibility in turn and try to eliminate every one but the right one. The latter will be the one you cannot cross out for any reason.

Your key sentence is the one beginning "Drying foods dates back . . ."

1—You cross it out because dehydration is not a method of preparing food for troops only. If you accept this you are *reading into* the paragraph.
2—You cannot cross this out at the moment. It *is mentioned,* it is *not read into,* and it is *not contradictory.*
3—You cross this one out because you would be *reading into* the paragraph. Dehydration is a food (not a packaging) process.
4—You eliminate this one again for the *reading into* reason. Keeping food dry (for example, in a sealed container) is quite different from drying foods to preserve them. Food that is not dehydrated can be kept dry.
5—This one is crossed out because it is *not mentioned* as the reason for dehydration. Certainly no flavor is added by the process, and the paragraph says that some is lost.

Thus your final choice is 2, the one you could not cross out for good reason.

3. OTHER FEATURES

As noted earlier, most questions testing reading comprehension will concentrate on main ideas and supporting details. However, there may also be some dealing with a writer's purpose, point of view, reliability, implied meanings, or style. Unless a question directs your attention to a particular word, phrase, or sentence—as is possible with implied meanings—you can assume that your final choice should relate to the test paragraph as a whole. For instance, you cannot properly evaluate style unless you consider the structure and language used throughout a selection, rather than just part of it. Questions on "other features" can still be handled by the *process of elimination*, as you will see in the analysis of the additional test paragraphs that follow.

Test Paragraph Interpretation—Example 2

(Includes question on writer's purpose)

If one is tempted to reflect on the type of language which is used in polite society, and, more particularly, if one is inclined to interpret it literally, one must conclude that social intercourse involves a collection of inanities and a tissues of lies. We say "Good morning" to the boss although the weather is foul and our temper is no better. We say "Pleased to meet you" when we really mean, "I hope I'll never see you again in my life." We chatter aimlessly at a tea about matters that are not fit to exercise the mind of a child of two.

To say "Pleased to meet you," or "Good morning" or to chatter at tea are examples of the ceremonial function of language. Language used in this way is not informational. It simply celebrates whatever feelings are responsible for bringing men together in social groups. It is said that the custom of shaking hands originated when primitive men held out empty hands to indicate that they had no concealed weapons and were thus amicably disposed. In the same way, when we say "How do you do" or "Good morning," we perform a sort of ceremony to indicate community of feeling with the person so addressed.

Questions

The title below that best expresses the ideas of the paragraph is:

1. The dishonesty of our daily language
2. The ceremonial use of language
3. Reflections on polite society
4. Primitive customs compared with modern customs
5. The value of language in winning social success

Elimination Process

Key words: *ceremonial language*

Eliminate:

1—contains only one of key words
3—contains neither key word
4—not really discussed
5—not mentioned

Answer: 2

The chief *purpose* of the author seems to be to:

1. ridicule society
2. amuse the reader

3. express a grudge against society
4. explain the basis of social conversation
5. explain the origin of language used in daily life

Elimination Process

Eliminate:

1—Here is a good example of why the whole paragraph must be considered. It does seem as if the writer is poking fun at society in his opening sentence, but the key phrase is "interpret it literally." In the rest of the paragraph, the writer clearly indicates that he is not being "literal" in his interpretation and understands the reasons for seemingly meaningless expressions. Hence, this possibility is actually contradictory.

2—Although some of the opening statements are amusing, it is not the "chief" purpose of the writer, rather only part of a serious analysis

3—read into, at best

5—not really discussed

Answer: 4

Test Paragraph Interpretation—Example 3

(Includes question on implied meaning)

Such homely virtues as thrift, hard work, and simplicity appear old-fashioned in these days. So probably we do well to remember the career of Benjamin Franklin, a true American. Though he had slight formal education, he became one of the best-educated men of his day, for he discovered the simple principle that one learns only what he teaches himself. Teachers can direct and organize the search for skills and information; a few can inspire. There is no substitute for the drudgery of learning. Franklin learned a trade and began reading inspirational books. He sought self-reliance and expressed thoughts that have interested more than one generation of readers. His essays and his autobiography reveal that his knowledge was useful.

Questions

The phrase that best expresses the main idea of the passage is:

1. The life of Benjamin Franklin
2. Teachers as educators
3. Formal education
4. The difficulties and satisfactions of self-education
5. The search for skill

Elimination Process

Key words: *self-education*

> (Note that Benjamin Franklin, although mentioned several times, is used only to serve as an example for illustrating the main idea.)

Eliminate:

1 and 5—neither key word present
2 and 3—at best only part of the main idea

Answer: 4

An *implied meaning* in this selection is that:

1. old-fashioned virtues should be discarded
2. most people have the homely virtues
3. everyone can get an education

4. learning need not be drudgery
5. Franklin learned his trade by studying inspirational books

Elimination Process

Eliminate:

1, 2, and 4—Contradictory in terms of what is said in
      the selection

5—Obviously no cause and effect relationship here,
    hence, "read into," if chosen

Answer: 3

Test Paragraph Interpretation—Example 4

(Includes questions on style)

If Shakespeare needs any excuse for the exuberance of his language (the high key in which he pitched most of his dramatic dialogue), it should be remembered that he was doing on the plastic stage of his own day what on the pictorial stage of our day is not so much required. Shakespeare's dramatic figures stood out on a platform-stage, without background, with the audience on three sides of it. And the whole of his atmosphere and environment had to come from the gestures and language of the actors. When they spoke, they provided their own scenery, which we now provide for them. They had to do a good deal more (when they spoke) than actors have to do today in order to give the setting. They carried the scenery on their backs, as it were, and spoke it in words.

Questions

The phrase that best expresses the contents of the paragraph is:

1. The scenery of the Elizabethan stage
2. The importance of actors in Shakespearean drama
3. The influence of the Elizabethan stage on Shakespeare's style
4. The importance of words
5. Suitable gestures for the Elizabethan stage

Elimination Process

Key words: *Shakespeare's style*

Eliminate:

1, 2, and 5—only part of the main idea
4—not mentioned

Answer: 3

The nature of the stage for which Shakespeare wrote made it necessary for him to:

1. employ only highly dramatic situations
2. depend on scenery owned by the actors
3. have the actors shift the scenery
4. create atmosphere through the dialogue
5. restrict backgrounds to familiar types of scenes

Elimination Process

Eliminate:

1, 2, 3, and 5—not mentioned!

Answer: 4

Test Paragraph Interpretation—Example 5

(Includes questions on point of view and reliability)

It is no secret that I am not one of those naturalists who suffer from cities, or affect to do so, nor do I find a city unnatural or uninteresting, or a rubbish heap of follies. It has always seemed to me that there is something more than mechanically admirable about a train that arrives on time, a fire department that comes when you call it, a light that leaps into a room at a touch, and a clinic that will fight for the health of a penniless man and mass for him the agencies of mercy, the X-ray, the precious radium, the anesthetics, and the surgical skill. For, beyond any pay these services receive, stands out the pride in perfect performance. And above all, I admire the noble impersonality of civilization that does not inquire where the recipient stands on religion, or politics, or race. I call this beauty, and I call it spirit—not some mystical soulfulness that nobody can define, but the spirit of man that has been a million years a-growing.

Questions

The title below that best expresses the ideas of this paragraph is:

1. The spirit of the city
2. Advantages of a city home
3. Disagreements among naturalists
4. Admirable characteristics of cities
5. Tolerance in the city

Elimination Process

Key words: *admire cities*

Eliminate:

> 2—not mentioned
> 1, 3, and 5—only partially suggested or mentioned; also
> key word missing in 3

Answer: 4

From the writer's point of view, the most admirable aspect of city life is its:

1. punctuality
2. free benefits
3. impartial service
4. mechanical improvements
5. health clinics

Elimination Process

Eliminate:

> The key to answering this question rests with your being able to tie in the words "most admirable" in the question with "above all" in the next-to-last sentence of the paragraph.
>
> 1, 2, 4, and 5—Although all these are referred to or implied, not one fits the "most admirable" label.

Answer: 3

The writer's opinion commands great respect because it is:

1. based on statistics
2. written so well
3. shared by all naturalists
4. contrary to that of suburbanites
5. unusually favorable, coming from a naturalist

Eliminate:

    1 and 4—not mentioned
    3—contradictory
    2—not relevant for judging reliability

Answer: 5

Sample Test A

Now you can try your skill in using the elimination process on the following set of reading comprehension exercises taken from a state examination in Comprehensive English. In the set, the total credits for the answers add up to 20, each "title" question being worth 2 points, and the others, 1 each. A final score of 15 is average, 16–18, good, and 19–20, excellent.

Paragraph A

I have heard it suggested that the "upper class" English accent has been of value in maintaining the British Empire and Commonwealth. The argument runs that all manner of folk in distant places, understanding the English language, will catch in this accent the notes of tradition, pride, and authority and so will be suitably impressed. This might have been the case some five or six decades ago but it is certainly not true today. The accent is more likely to be a liability than an asset.

It is significant that the Royal Family in their speeches and broadcasts use a considerably modified form of the accent. The public English of George V was magnificently free from all affectations. His chil-

dren and grandchildren have done their best to follow his example.

(Insert the numbers of your choices in the parentheses.)

The title below that best expresses the ideas of this
passage is:

    1. The "King's English"
    2. The affected language of royalty
    3. The decline of the British Empire
    4. Changed effects of "British accent"
    5. Preventing the spread of Cockney .... (   )

According to the author, the "upper class" English
accent:

    1. has been imitated all over the world
    2. may have helped to perpetuate the British Empire
       before 1900
    3. has been strongly opposed by British royalty
    4. has brought about the destruction of the British
       Commonwealth
    5. may have caused arguments in distant corners of
       the Empire .... (   )

Paragraph B

We were about a quarter mile away when quiet
swept over the colony. A thousand or more heads
periscoped. Two thousand eyes glared. Save for our
wading, the world's business had stopped. A thousand avian personalities were concentrated on us,
and the psychological force of this was terrific. Con-
tingents of homecoming feeders, suddenly aware of

four strange specks moving across the lake, would bank violently and speed away. Then the chain reaction began. Every throat in that rookery let go with a concatenation of wild, raspy, terrorized trumpet bursts. With all wings now fully spread and churning, and quadrupling the color mass, the birds began to move as one, and the sky was filled with the sound of judgment day.

Questions

The title below that best expresses the ideas of this passage is:

1. Our shore birds
2. A quiet colony
3. Judgment day
4. Waiting
5. An unwelcome intrusion upon a bird colony
   .... ( )

The passage indicates that the writer:

1. was a psychologist
2. observed the fear of the flying birds
3. was terrified at the sounds
4. crossed the lake by boat
5. went alone to the rookery .... ( )

According to the passage, when they first noticed the visitors, the birds of the colony:

1. flew away
2. became very quiet
3. churned their wings
4. set up a series of cries
5. glared at the homecoming birds .... ( )

Paragraph C

Today in America vast concourses of youth are flocking to our colleges, eager for something, just what they do not know. It makes much difference what they get. They will be prone to demand something they can immediately use; the tendency is strong to give it to them; science, economics, business administration, law in its narrower sense. I submit that the shepherds should not first feed the flocks with these. I argue for the outlines of what used to go as a liberal education—not necessarily in the sense that young folks should waste precious years in efforts, unsuccessful for some reason I cannot understand, to master ancient tongues; but I speak for an introduction into the thoughts and deeds of men who have lived before them, in other countries than their own, with other strifes and other needs. This I maintain, not in the interest of that general cultural background, which is so often a cloak for the superior person, the prig, the snob and the pedant. But I submit to you that in some such way alone can we meet and master the highpower salesman of political patent medicines.

Questions

The title below that best expresses the ideas of this passage is:

1. Why pupils go to college
2. Foreign languages for culture
3. The need for vocational training
4. The shepherd and his student flock
5. The importance of a liberal education . . . . . ( )

One purpose of a college education should be to help students to:

1. achieve political wisdom
2. become good salesmen
3. develop their talents
4. find their individual interests
5. become future leaders .... ( )

Many students entering college desire to study:

1. other countries
2. history and law
3. cultural subjects
4. "practical" subjects
5. too many subjects .... ( )

The writer stresses the study of:

1. other cultures
2. foreign languages
3. politics and medicine
4. business administration
5. general cultures .... ( )

Paragraph D

Your mind, like your body, is a thing whereof the powers are developed by effort. That is a principal use, as I see it, of hard work in studies. Unless you train your body you can't be an athlete, and unless you train your mind you can't be much of a scholar. The four miles an oarsman covers at top speed is in itself nothing to the good, but the physical capacity to hold out over the course is thought of be of some worth. So a good part of what you learn by hard study may not be permanently retained, and may not seem to be of much final value, but your mind is a better and more powerful instrument because you have learned it. "Knowledge is power," but still more the faculty of acquiring and using knowledge is power. If you have a trained and powerful mind, you are bound to have stored it with something, but its value is more in what it can do, what it can grasp and use, than in what it contains, and if it were possible, as it is not, to come out of college with a trained and disciplined mind and nothing useful in it, you would still be ahead, and still, in a manner, educated.

Questions

The title below that best expresses the ideas of this passage is:

1. "Knowledge is power"
2. How to retain and use facts
3. Why acquire knowledge
4. Physical and mental effort
5. The trained mind .... ( )

The author emphasizes that many of the facts you acquire by hard study:

1. deal with rules of health
2. will be forgotten
3. are of questionable value
4. will be very useful to you in later life
5. will help you to understand the meaning of life
   .... ( )

The man leaving college with a disciplined mind:

1. is certain to succeed
2. is likely to be a poor athlete
3. has finished his education

4. is educated
5. can grasp any problem .... (   )

Paragraph E

The total impression made by any work of fiction cannot be rightly understood without a sympathetic perception of the artistic aims of the writer. Consciously or unconsciously, he has accepted certain facts, and rejected or suppressed other facts, in order to give unity to the particular aspect of human life which he is depicting. No novelist possesses the impartiality, the indifference, the infinite tolerance of Nature. Nature displays to us, with complete unconcern, the beautiful and the ugly, the precious and the trivial, the pure and the impure. But a writer must select the aspects of Nature and human nature that are demanded by the work in hand. He is forced to select, to combine, to create.

Questions

The title below that best expresses the ideas of this paragraph is:

1. Unity in disunity
2. The tolerance and impartiality of Nature
3. The novelist's failure
4. Understanding fiction
5. Nature, the true novelist .... (   )

A novelist chooses for his story material which will:

1. prove his impartiality
2. further his general purpose
3. completely copy Nature
4. create a beautiful effect
5. display his unconcern .... (   )

A reader must:

1. detect trivialities
2. understand all aspects of Nature
3. discover the aim of the novelist
4. maintain a tolerant attitude
5. reject certain facts . . . . ( )

ANSWERS: A. 4, 2;   B. 5, 2, 2;   C. 5, 1, 4, 1;
           D. 5, 2, 4;   E. 4, 2, 3.

Sample Test B

The paragraphs that follow were taken from various examinations offered by the United States Civil Service Commission. Continue to use the elimination process to guide you in making the proper choices from among the possibilities.

1. "The application of the steam engine to the sawmill changed the whole lumber industry. Formerly the mills remained near the streams; now they follow the timber. Formerly the logs were floated downstream to their destination; now they are carried by the railroads."

What besides the method of transportation does the quotation indicate has changed in the lumber industry?

    a. speed of cutting lumber
    b. location of market
    c. type of timber sold
    d. route of railroads
    e. source of power .... ( )

2. "More patents have been issued for inventions relating to transportation than for those in any other

line of human activity. These inventions have re-
sulted in a great financial saving to the people and
have made possible a civilization that could not have
existed without them."

Select the alternative that is best supported by the
quotation. Transportation

    a. would be impossible without inventions
    b. is an important factor in our civilization
    c. is still to be much improved
    d. is more important than any other activity
    e. is carried on through the Patent Office . . . . . (   )

3. "There exists a false but popular idea that a clue
is some mysterious fact which most people overlook,
but which some very keen investigator easily dis-
covers and recognizes as having, in itself, a remarkable meaning. The clue is most often an ordinary fact
which an observant person picks up—something
which gains its significance when, after a long series
of careful investigations, it is connected with a net-
work of other clues."

According to the quotation, to be of value, clues must
be

    a. discovered by skilled investigators
    b. found under mysterious circumstances
    c. discovered soon after the crime
    d. observed many times
    e. connected with other facts . . . . (   )

4. "Just as the procedure of a collection department
must be clear-cut and definite, the steps being taken
with the sureness of a skilled chess player, so the

various paragraphs of a collection letter must show clear organization, giving evidence of a mind that, from the beginning, has had a specific end in view."

The quotation best supports the view that a collection letter should always

    a. show a spirit of sportsmanship
    b. be divided into several paragraphs
    c. express confidence in the debtor
    d. be brief, but courteous
    e. be carefully planned .... ( )

5. "The likelihood of America's exhausting her natural resources seems to be growing less. All kinds of waste are being reworked and new uses are constantly being found for almost everything. We are getting more use out of our goods and are making many new by-products out of what was formerly thrown away."

The quotation best supports the statement that we seem to be in less danger of exhausting our resources because

    a. economy is found to lie in the use of substitutes
    b. more service is obtained from a given amount of material
    c. more raw materials are being produced
    d. supply and demand are being controlled
    e. we are allowing time for nature to restore them
    .... ( )

6. "Probably few people realize, as they drive on a concrete road, that steel is used to keep the surface flat and even, in spite of the weight of buses and trucks. Steel bars, deeply imbedded in the concrete, provide sinews to take the stresses so that they cannot crack the slab or make it wavy."

The quotation best supports the statement that a concrete road

    a. is expensive to build
    b. usually cracks under heavy weights
    c. looks like any other road
    d. is used exclusively for heavy traffic
    e. is reinforced with other material .... ( )

7. "The countries in the Western Hemisphere were settled by people who were ready each day for new adventure. The peoples of North and South America have retained, in addition to expectant and forward-looking attitudes, the ability and the willingness that they have often shown in the past to adapt themselves to new conditions."

The quotation best supports the statement that the peoples in the Western Hemisphere

    a. no longer have fresh adventures daily
    b. are capable of making changes as new situations arise
    c. are no more forward-looking than the peoples of other regions
    d. tend to resist regulations
    e. differ considerably among themselves ..... ( )

8. "The coloration of textile fabrics composed of cotton and wool generally requires two processes, as the process used in dyeing wool is seldom capable of fixing the color upon cotton. The usual method is to immerse the fabric in the requisite baths to dye the

263

wool and then to treat the partially dyed material in the manner found suitable for cotton."

The quotation best supports the statement that the dyeing of textile fabrics composed of cotton and wool

    a. is less complicated than the dyeing of wool alone
    b. is more successful when the material contains more cotton than wool
    c. is not satisfactory when solid colors are desired
    d. is restricted to two colors for any one fabric
    e. is usually based upon the methods required for dyeing the different materials .... ( )

9. "Every language has its peculiar word associations that have no basis in logic and cannot therefore be reasoned about. These idiomatic expressions are ordinarily acquired only by much reading and conversation although questions about such matters may sometimes be answered by the dictionary. Dictionaries large enough to include quotations from standard authors are especially serviceable in determining questions of idiom."

The quotation best supports the statement that idiomatic expressions

    a. give rise to meaningless arguments
    b. are widely used by recognized authors
    c. are explained in most dictionaries
    d. are more common in some languages than in others
    e. are best learned by observation of the language as actually used .... ( )

10. "The telegraph networks of the country now constitute wonderfully operated institutions, affording for ordinary use of modern business an important means of communication. The transmission of messages by electricity has reached the goal for which the postal service has long been striving, namely, the elimination of distance as an effective barrier of communication."

The quotation best supports the statement that

a. a new standard of communication has been attained
b. in the telegraph service, messages seldom go astray
c. it is the distance between the parties which creates the need for communication
d. modern business relies more upon the telegraph than upon the mails
e. the telegraph is a form of postal service ... ( )

ANSWERS: 1. e,   2. b,   3. e,   4. e,   5. b;   6. e,   7. b,
            8. e,   9. e,   10. a.

Score 2 points for each correct answer. You did well if your total was 16 or better.

Sample Test C

The College Entrance Examination Board (CEEB) prepares the Scholastic Aptitude Test (SAT) and other examinations that are taken every year by thousands of students who are planning to enter college. The Scholastic Aptitude Test measures various kinds of ability in two broad areas, Verbal and Mathematics. A 30-minute Standard Written English Test (SWET) is also included to measure the applicant's ability to write in a clear and organized fashion.

It is significant to note that about 50% of the time devoted to the verbal parts of the test concerns reading comprehension. You should find it interesting to test your skill with the typical examples of reading questions reprinted from *A Description of the College Board Scholastic Aptitude Test*. Should you desire a complete explanation of the SAT, plus valuable suggestions for handling various types of questions, you can obtain the latest booklet by writing to the College Entrance Examination Board, P.O. Box 592, Princeton, New Jersey 08540; or to Box 1025, Berkeley, California 94701. A more detailed description of entrance and qualifying examinations, including sample questions and answers, can be obtained from a variety of booklets published by book companies that specialize in such materials. Your local book shop should be able to provide a list of available titles and secure copies of booklets you wish to study.

Good evidence that full comprehension is the essence of superior reading ability is found in that portion of one of the early College Board booklets that explain the types of questions asked:

"Reading comprehension is tested at several levels. Some of the questions depend simply on the understanding of the plain sense of what has been directly stated. To answer other questions, you must be able to interpret and analyze what you have read. Still other questions are designed to test your ability to recognize reasonable applications of the principles or opinions expressed by the author. And some of the questions require you to judge what you have read—to observe good and bad points in the presentation, to recognize how far the author has supported his statements by evidence, to recognize and evaluate the means used by the author to get his points across, and so on."

Directions: Each passage in this section is followed by questions based on its content. After reading a passage, choose the best answer among the five suggested answers to the question.

Passage

Talking with a young man about success and a career, Doctor Samuel Johnson advised the youth "to know something about everything and everything about something." The advice was good—in Doctor Johnson's day, when London was like an isolated village and it took a week to get the news from Paris, Rome, or Berlin. Today, if a man were to take all knowledge for his province and try to know something about everything, the allotment of time would give one minute to each subject, and soon the youth would flit from topic to topic as a butterfly from flower to flower, and life would be as evanescent as the butterfly that lives for the present honey and moment. Today commercial, literary, or inventive success means concentration.

55. The author implies that a modern scientist

    A. makes discoveries by accident
    B. must bend his mind in a specific direction
    C. is able to contribute only if he has a background of general knowledge
    D. must be well-versed in the arts
    E. must be successful, whatever the cost ... ( )

56. According to the passage, if we tried now to follow Dr. Johnson's advice, we would

    A. lead a more worthwhile life
    B. have a slower-paced, more peaceful, and more productive life
    C. fail in our attempts
    D. hasten the progress of civilization
    E. perceive a deeper reality .... ( )

57. Why does the author compare the youth to a butterfly?

    A. Butterflies symbolize a life of luxury and ease.
    B. The butterfly, like the youth, exhausts a present source of energy.
    C. The butterfly, like the youth, has no clear single objective.

D. The butterfly, like the youth, is unaware of the future.

E. The butterfly lives but a short time and thus retains the innocence of youth .... ( )

58. In which one of the following comparisons made by the author is the parallelism of the elements least satisfactory?

A. Topics and flowers
B. The youth and the butterfly
C. London and an isolated village
D. Knowledge and province
E. Life and the butterfly .... ( )

Passage

Birds always seem intensely alive because of their high body temperature and the agility that comes of flight. But being intensely alive does not necessarily mean being intensely intelligent, as we know from human examples. In respect to their minds just as much as their bodies, birds have developed along other lines than mammals. Mammals have gradually perfected intelligence and the capacity for learning by experience until this line has culminated in that conscious reason and in that deliberate reliance upon the accumulated experience of previous generations which are unique properties of the human species. Among mammals the level of intelligence has gradually risen, and simultaneously the power and fixity of instincts has diminished. Birds, on the other hand, have kept instinct as the mainstay of their behavior, although, like all other backboned animals, they possess some intelligence and some power of profiting by experience. These are subordinate, however, used merely to polish up the outfit of instincts which is provided by heredity without having to be paid for in terms of experience. Indeed, the anatomist could support these observations by comparing the brains of birds and mammals. For whereas in mammals we can trace a steady increase in the size and elaboration of the cerebral hemispheres, the front part of the brain which we know to be the seat of intelligence and learning, this region is never highly developed in any birds, but remains relatively small without convolutions on its surface. Other parts of the brain which are known to be the regulating machinery for complicated but more automatic and more emotional actions are in birds relatively larger than in the four-footed creatures.

59. The intelligence of birds is inherently limited by their

    A. small cerebral hemispheres
    B. extreme agility
    C. well-developed instincts
    D. small range of experience
    E. high body temperature .... ( )

60. It can be inferred from the passage that the degree of activity in a given animal is related to

    A. size of cerebral hemispheres
    B. number of cerebral convolutions
    C. accumulated experience
    D. body temperature
    E. lack of intelligence .... ( )

61. According to the author, instinctive action in birds is

    A. unaffected by learning
    B. independent of conscious reason

C. dependent upon intelligence
D. a measure of their intelligence
E. controlled by the cerebral hemispheres .. (   )

62. The words *accumulated experience,* as used in the fourth sentence, could properly imply all of the following EXCEPT

A. language
B. science
C. manual dexterity
D. social organization
E. legal codes .... (   )

63. An ambiguity exists in the last sentence because the author fails to consider the fact that

A. mammals are also emotional creatures
B. not all four-footed creatures are mammals
C. some birds do not need a regulating machinery
D. small birds have relatively smaller regulating centers
E. mammals also carry on automatic actions .... (   )

Passage

Most professional economists today would agree that the primary purpose of economics is analytical, to *discover what is.* Whatever other aims some of them may have, their chief concern is to establish the principles upon which the present economic system works. There is a school of thought which regards economics as capable of becoming as exact and as "universally valid" as the physical sciences, and which denies, by implication, its essentially social and historical nature. These views, however, are put forward only on the occasion of methodological discussion and do not seem to affect the scope of the bulk of the work of members of this school: they are still mainly interested in the working of present-day capitalism.

The general public is very rarely aware of this positive and analytical purpose which the professional regards as the paramount, or even as the only legitimate one. The public knows that it can justifiably demand of the economist a statement of how the system works (though its faith in the explanation which is forthcoming is seldom great); but it generally wants to know also what is the right thing to *do*. Economists cannot always shirk this question; and when they answer they reveal more far-reaching differences of opinion than any that arise in the positive analysis upon which they all claim to base their advice.

78. The passage implies that economists try to avoid answering the question

    A. What is the right thing to do?
    B. How can a positive analysis be made?
    C. What is the purpose of economics?
    D. What is actually true?
    E. How does the economic system work? ... ( )

79. It can be inferred from the passage that the author believes economics to be

    A. an exact science
    B. social and historical in nature
    C. a highly methodological discipline
    D. primarily capitalistic in function
    E. basically altruistic .... ( )

80. In which one of the following would the "school of thought" in the third sentence be most likely to find expression?

    A. Radio round-table discussions
    B. Government bulletins
    C. Political speeches
    D. Popular magazines
    E. Professional journals .... ( )

81. The passage implies that the opinions of economists differ most with respect to the

    A. basic facts with which economics should deal
    B. basic purpose of economics
    C. means for achieving social goals
    D. methods by which facts are to be gathered
    E. positive analysis upon which economic advice is taken .... ( )

Passage

The best excuse that can be made for avarice is that it generally prevails in old men or in men of cold tempers, where all the other affections are extinct; and the mind, being incapable of remaining without some passion or pursuit, at least finds out this monstrously absurd one, which suits the coldness and inactivity of its temper. At the same time, it seems very extraordinary that so frosty, spiritless a passion should be able to carry us further than all the warmth of youth and pleasure. But if we look more narrowly into the matter, we shall find that this very circumstance renders the explication of the case more easy.

When the temper is warm and full of vigor, it naturally shoots out more ways than one and produces inferior passions to counterbalance, in some degree, its predominant inclination. It is impossible for a person of that temper, however bent on any pursuit, to be deprived of all sense of shame or all regard to sentiments of mankind. His friends must have some influence over him; and other considerations are apt to have their weight. All this serves to restrain him within some bounds. But it is no wonder that the avaricious man, being, from the coldness of his temper, without regard to reputation, to friendship, or to pleasure, should be carried so far by his prevailing inclination and should display his passion in such surprising instances.

We find no vice so irreclaimable as avarice and for this reason I am more apt to approve of those who attack it with wit and humor than of those who treat it in a serious manner. I would have the rest of mankind at least diverted by our manner of exposing it; as indeed there is no kind of diversion of which they seem so willing to partake.

82. The author implies that most people are *not* avaricious because avarice

    A. can easily be detected by observers

    B. is an absurd pursuit

    C. rarely leads to success

    D. can be prevented by even a small sense of shame

    E. can be cured by persistent and witty attacks
               . . . . ( )

83. In the last sentence of the second paragraph, *coldness* is used to mean

    A. senility

    B. anger

C. irascibility

D. stupidity

E. callousness .... ( )

84. The author observes that men generally are willing to look at avarice in order to

    A. admire its surprising success

    B. enjoy criticizing it

    C. imitate it

    D. profit by its errors

    E. guard against it .... ( )

85. The author would disapprove of those who seriously attack avarice since they

    A. waste their efforts

    B. unconsciously increase its importance

    C. do not really understand its origin

    D. do so only to entertain and not to reform

    E. use methods which are too mild .... ( )

ANSWERS: 55. B, 56. C, 57. C, 58. E, 59. A; 60. D, 61. B, 62. C, 63. B, 78. A; 79. B, 80. E, 81. C, 82. D, 83. E; 84. B, 85. A.

Notes on the more difficult questions

58. The least satisfactory comparison is E. What the author really means is that human life would be like the *life* of a butterfly—aimless and evanescent—not that human life would be like the butterfly itself.

61. The answer is B, since the author says that conscious reason is unique to the human species—possessed by humans alone. A is incorrect because the author says that birds do learn (profit by experience) and that the learning polishes up the outfit of instincts.

63. The answer is B. The author begins by comparing mammals with birds. But when he varies his vocabulary with *four-footed creatures,* his statement becomes unclear; there are some four-footed creatures that are not mammals (lizard, turtle, etc.).

80. The answer is E because "methodological discussion" suggests that when one economist talks to another, through the medium of a professional journal, he is likely to advance theories that he would not necessarily proclaim to the general public. All the remaining possibilities refer to areas in which the public would be the principal audience.

81. The answer is C because the key phrase in the passage here is "wants to know also what is the right thing to *do.*" This is another way of saying that information is desired regarding the means of achieving social goals.

84. The answer is B because the author says that in so far as exposing avarice is concerned "there is no kind of diversion of which they seem so willing to partake."

85. The first sentence in the last paragraph is the key to answer A because the author states that "no vice [is] so irreclaimable as avarice." Obviously it would be wasted effort to attempt to influence seriously a characteristic that is almost impossible to change.

If you were able to answer 14 or more of the questions correctly, you can congratulate yourself on having done well on this set. It is important to point out that if you were able to handle the SAT passages satisfactorily you proved to yourself that you are capable not only of picking out main ideas and details in your reading but also of using judgment and analysis—both so necessary for full comprehension!

FINAL READING INVENTORY

No Roadblocks!
Stretched Recognition Span!
Speed Adjusted to Purpose and Material!
Full Comprehension!
Enlarged Vocabulary!
Skimming, When Necessary!
Extensive Reading of Varied Materials!

DALE CARNEGIE—THE MAN WHO HAS HELPED MILLIONS TO GREATER ACHIEVEMENT—CAN HELP YOU!

Start enjoying your job, your personal relationships—every aspect of your life— more fully with these classic books. Check the ones you want and use the coupon below to order.

_____ 47212-7   HOW TO DEVELOP SELF-CONFIDENCE AND INFLUENCE PEOPLE BY PUBLIC SPEAKING $3.50

_____ 49269-1   HOW TO ENJOY YOUR LIFE AND YOUR JOB $2.95

_____ 49165-2   HOW TO STOP WORRYING AND START LIVING $3.50

_____ 49891-6   THE QUICK AND EASY WAY TO EFFECTIVE SPEAKING $3.50